FACING THE BROKENNESS

Meditations for Parents of Sexually Abused Children

K·C·RIDINGS

Pam & Sheldon,

May this book strengthen and increase
your courage for your journey of healing.
we pray that you'll continue to uncover

HERALD PRESS
Scottdale, Pennsylvania
Waterloo, Ontario

how your faith
can help you
through the brokeness
of this experience

Sonja & Darcy

Library of Congress Cataloging-in-Publication Data
Ridings, K. C., 1947-
  Facing the brokenness : meditations for parents of sexually abused
children / K. C. Ridings.
    p.   cm.
  ISBN 0-8361-3573-3
  1. Parents of sexually abused children—Prayer-books and
devotions—English. I. Title.
BV4596.P37R53   1991
242'.645—dc20   91-30239
                                                                     CIP

The paper used in this publication is recycled and meets the minimum
requirements of American National Standard for Information Sciences—
Permanence of Paper for Printed Library Materials, ANSI Z39.48-1984.

See other Notes and Credits on pages 173-174.

FACING THE BROKENNESS
Copyright © 1991 by Herald Press, Scottdale, Pa. 15683
    Published simultaneously in Canada by Herald Press,
        Waterloo, Ont. N2L 6H7. All rights reserved.
Library of Congress Catalog Number: 91-30239
International Standard Book Number: 0-8361-3573-3
Printed in the United States of America
Book design and inside art by Gwen Stamm
Cover art by Paula Johnson and Gwen Stamm

99 98 97 96 95 94 93 92 91 10 9 8 7 6 5 4 3 2 1

*I want to express publicly before God's people
my heartfelt thanks to God for his mighty miracles.
All who are thankful should ponder them with me.
For God's miracles demonstrate his honor,
majesty, and eternal goodness.*

Psalm 111:1-3, TLB adapted

Contents

HEALING THE HURTING CHILD

HEAR THE CRY OF PEOPLE SUFFERING

CHRISTIAN RESPONSE TO CHILD SEXUAL ABUSE

Foreword

"Think about these things" (Phil. 4:8).

These meditations reflect the author's personal pilgrimage through feelings of anger, pain, brokenness, compassion, and forgiveness—toward healing. It took great courage to share each piece of her brokenness. Through facing what happened and by writing each page, she brought the secrets of the unspeakable into the open. This facilitated closure and brought healing to the brokenness. The author, in a skillful and insightful way, captured many of the agonies both victims and offenders experience.

This book stands out as a rare contribution to understanding the complexities surrounding this emotional subject. I know of no other work that dares so honestly to address the issue that surely faces the household of faith in this day of public outcry about child sexual abuse. The author's research is thorough and factual. It is a dynamic and comprehensive treatment of a "silent subject."

People of faith don't want to talk about it. Tradition has told us, "It's not nice to talk about sex or sexual deviations." It is unthinkable even to suggest that some behavior, within the family or among friends or realtives, was sexual abuse. The author challenges the reader and the household of faith to "face the broken-

6

ness," acknowledge with courage the reality of child sexual abuse, and talk about it openly and honestly.

You, too, can live this pilgrimage with the author.

It takes courage to make the journey.

You cannot ponder these pages and remain untouched. You cannot meditate on "these things" without identifying with the author, or someone you know and care about. While *Facing the Brokenness* speaks specifically to parents of a sexually abused child, there is material for meditation and direction for healing for each person involved, for both victim and offender.

You may be:

- A parent or grandparent of a sexually abused child.
- An adult survivor of child sexual abuse.
- An offender, charged and convicted, or still offending.
- A victim, friend of a victim, or offender.
- A member of a church where victim or offender is also a member.
- A church leader or Sunday school teacher.

Facing the Brokenness will be useful as a private and personal experience, for a study-and-discussion group, or for a sex-offender treatment group.

May each reader experience the courage to face the brokenness brought about through child sexual abuse.

—Theron Weldy, Psychotherapist
Sex Offender Treatment
Phoenix, Arizona

Preface

I frequented Christian bookstores for years hoping to find material to meet the special needs of our child and family. As the soft music played and children roamed back and forth in the aisles, I made my embarrassed request to the clerk. "Please, can you tell me if you have any books for children who have been sexually abused?"

In the early years of my search, the clerk usually looked at me with lowered eyebrows and glanced up and down my body before answering my question. The answer was always the same. "No, we don't carry anything like that."

As adult survivors of sexual abuse broke years of silence, I became more hopeful. I returned to the Christian bookstores looking for material to help my child. Maybe the clerks had become used to hearing the words sexual abuse in a Christian bookstore because their body language changed. Now they cheerfully pointed to the coloring book and children's storybook on sexual abuse prevention.

I remember looking at one clerk and telling her, "It's too late for that now. I need a book on how my faith can help my wounded child and hurting family today."

The discouragement I felt showed through my watery eyes. Her words stayed with me for years. "Other people have come in asking for help and reading material. The only thing I can tell them is that the church is not ready to admit sexual abuse can happen to Christians."

National figures on sexual abuse tell us two out of four girls and one out of seven boys are molested before adulthood. What I find more shocking is that four out of every eight parents could be parenting a girl who is a victim of sexual abuse and two in fourteen parents could be parenting a boy who is a victim of sexual abuse. There is no magic line that protects Christian households and their children from this sin of sexual violence that is running rampant in our society. The sexual abusers of children are often men. Yet researchers are finding more mothers who sexually victimized their children or were silent and denying while suspecting or knowing about abuse of their child.

There is a popular and persistent misconception that those who are survivors of sexual abuse will somehow outgrow it or be able to put the past behind them when they get older. Many Christians minimize the violence done to the victim, believing all a survivor has to do is forgive and forget. You have only to ask parents if their sexually abused child has been miraculously healed. Parents of victims tell us again and again, "I'm still trying to get my child just to talk about the abuse and the effects it is having on her life today."

Parents can be wonderful support persons and a place of refuge for a hurting child, but they should never be primary therapists for a sexual abuse victim. In an effort to assist our child in facing her past, we located a competent sexual abuse therapist. At the same time I began to address the impact I had as a parent with my child's recovery. I identified the conflicts *I* was having and began to work on *my* feelings.

This book is not a therapy book. Instead, it is a devotional book with questions for reflection to help you identify your feelings, along with activities you can do as a parent to assist your sexually abused child. It also provides Scripture, prayers, sexual abuse education, and action plans taken from my private devotions as a parent of a sexual abuse victim. I want to address the many areas of childhood sexual abuse. In hope that readers can recognize their

9

situation, I have drawn on my experiences on the Christian Parents Help Line for Sexual Abuse.

Seven years have passed since we discovered our children were sexually abused before they were placed in our home for adoption. Our family is better and stronger for the courage shared and the creative methods we discovered to help our children.

Today our two daughters—with the assistance of therapy, family communication, and God's remarkable healing through his Word—are living examples that children can *begin* the journey to recover from sexual abuse inflicted upon them. Angelica and Marisol both supported this project and have contributed to the completion of this book. We admire their courage and are grateful to both of them for the depth of love they have added to our family. My husband, Joseph, and I feel very blessed.

Acknowledgments

I thank my children, who have taught me new definitions for courage, faith, and healing.

A word of gratitude is also due to the many men and women who called the Christian Parents Help Line for Sexual Abuse to ask for prayer and support.

A writer's thank you goes to Tempe Christian Writers Club, for without their loving support the following pages would not have been possible.

Thanks to Mennonite Central Committee for the resources in the packet, "Broken Boundaries," and to other authors pointing the way to recovery from sexual abuse (*see* Notes and Credits).

Finally, I extend my genuine appreciation to my husband for the help and encouragement he has given me with this manuscript. Thank you for understanding and helping me give my gift of writing to God's children.

—K. C. Ridings
Mesa, Arizona

How to Use the Book

These thirty-one days require active involvement on your part. While it is a devotional for reading, it is also a practical, experimental manual requiring your action. To profit fully from this book, you will need to carry out the actions you decide at the end of each worksheet.

Before you begin Day One, sit down and evaluate your schedule. You will need fifteen minutes daily for the next thirty-one days. This needs to be private time when you are alone with God, free from distractions and interruptions. If possible the workbook page should be completed at the same time you do the devotional. Thus you are making your verbal prayer into an action prayer.

You may find it hard to keep the enthusiasm you had when you first started the program, especially if your child or family is having some rough times right now. This is all the more reason to find a quiet corner in your home and identify it as your prayer corner. Your prayer corner can be anywhere you decide. My corner has changed locations several times. I have a friend who keeps a *portable* prayer corner on her bedroom dresser where she can retreat at a moment's notice. On a tray, she keeps her Bible, candle, matches, pens, markers, paper, devotional book, and journal.

This book also includes suggestions for symbols to be placed in your prayer corner. Almost all the symbols are household items or things that are easily made. The symbols are planned specifically for those times you are too overwhelmed to pray and believe. The symbol will remind you of the difficulty each of us has in living the gospel in our families. If you find yourself wanting to stay with a symbol, then move that symbol to another place in your home and continue on with the thirty-one meditations. After you finish the book, return to the devotionals in which you need additional healing. It was not unusual for me to use symbols for a month at a time, sometimes longer, sometimes shorter.

Finally, remember that following the example of Jesus is a life-long commitment requiring lifelong work. This thirty-one day devotional guide is not a crash-course manual you can do and then forget. It can help your wounded family members. But after you finish the book, you must continue making daily decisions to put God first in your life and in the center of your home. The best prayer corners are those that are used every day.

Don't hesitate to use this devotional book over and over again. Presented here are spiritual building blocks needed for families recovering from sexual abuse. When problems arise in the future, feel free to turn to the devotion that will help you.

There is no right or wrong way for the Holy Spirit to work or direct your life. If you find yourself returning to one devotion, it is probably an area of your life the Lord wants to heal. Allow the Lord to take all the time he needs to help bring peace and wholeness to yourself and your child.

My prayer for you is that God will greatly enrich and strengthen your family as he has done mine.

The Hurting Parent

The Lord is near to the brokenhearted,
and saves the crushed in spirit.
—Psalm 34:18

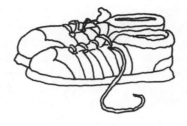

FIRST DAY

Walk in My Shoes

For the prayer corner: A pair of worn-out shoes.

Pilate, wanting to release Jesus, addressed them again; but they kept shouting, "Crucify, crucify him!" (Luke 23:20-21)

Read Luke 23:1-25.

When I held my child for the first time, I never suspected that my parenting role could change so drastically over the years. Things like adolescence and peer pressure were predictable changes which all parents face someday. Like most people, I thought sexual abuse happened to someone else's child. When it happened to my child, suddenly I was walking into an area of parenting I knew nothing about, and I was scared! I was frightened about the future. I was afraid for both myself and my child.

In 1983, sexual abuse was still fairly well hidden from society. In the library I found only two books on the subject. I felt embarrassed when I handed the woman the books to check out. After reading them, I felt an overwhelming sadness for my child. I was paralyzed with grief as I struggled with the knowledge that my daughter had been molested by a person she knew and trusted.

Well-meaning Christians told me prayer and forgiveness was the answer to any problem. As a Christian, I knew in my *mind* they were right, but in my *heart* I wasn't so sure any more. A betrayal this awful could not be made right with "forgive and forget."

As the months went by and the stress of parenting a sexually abused child became more evident, I came face to face with my own limitations and weakness. I neglected my daily reading of God's Word and I failed to walk in the footsteps of Jesus' example.

One day I was thinking how difficult it was to be in my shoes. I went to my closet and took out an old, nearly worn-out pair of shoes. That's the way I felt. I put the shoes on my nightstand. Every time I sat in front of those shoes, I had a pity party. "Isn't it awful?" "Isn't it terrible?" I'd say to myself.

As the shock of the disclosure wore off, I came face to face with a rage that filled every muscle in my body. I remember one day in particular my behavior was quite awful. Sitting in front of my shoes, with the tears streaming down my face, I realized I was kicking myself around and accusing myself: "Am I not an awful parent? Am I not a terrible Christian?"

I left the shoes on my nightstand for a long time. Their presence forced me to confront my innermost self. I spoke a one-sentence prayer. "Lord, heal me with Scripture and restore me for the purpose for which you made me." It didn't happen that day or the next, but I did find a Scripture that applied to my situation.

I recalled the road Jesus walked to Calvary, a road paved with fear, accusations, insults, and false judgments. Priests and religious leaders took Jesus to the palace of the Roman governor, Pontius Pilate. They wanted a judgment made against Jesus for treason. They demanded that a sentence of death be confirmed and carried out against Jesus. Pilate questioned Jesus several times. He did not believe Jesus had done wrong. The crowd's hostility rose to riot pitch, exploding in their clamor that Jesus be given the most brutal form of Roman execution: "Crucify him!"

I realized I was behaving like the hostile crowd. I was shaking my angry fist at my child, resenting her because she kept her secret hidden from us. I was blaming her for the things that happened to her. I was the judge and the jury. Yet inwardly I had concentrated my energy on my stumblings and failures. I liked the "better" parent I used to be before I knew the molestation occurred. No wonder I felt as though I were carrying the weight of the whole world on my shoulders. So I prayed.

"Lord, lift this judgmental spirit from me. Help me to be a peaceful and gentle person. Help me walk in your example."

Being the parent of a sexually abused child is a tremendous challenge. Sometimes I return to the closet, take out my shoes, and place them on my prayer corner table. They remind me to seek a closer walk with my Lord, even if he has to carry me.

My Daily Christian Walk

Blessed are the poor in spirit, for theirs is the kingdom of heaven.
Blessed are those who mourn, for they will be comforted.
Blessed are the meek, for they will inherit the earth.
Blessed are those who hunger and thirst for righteousness,
    for they will be filled.
Blessed are the merciful, for they will receive mercy.
Blessed are the pure in heart, for they will see God.
Blessed are the peacemakers, for they will be called children of God.
Blessed are those who are persecuted for righteousness' sake,
    for theirs is the kingdom of heaven.
Blessed are you when people revile you and persecute you and utter
all kinds of evil against you falsely on my account. (Matthew 5:3-11)

For Reflection

- Describe the pair of shoes you put in your prayer corner.

- What does God promise those who walk in the way of the Lord and follow Jesus? (Psalm 128:1-2)

Prayer of Commitment

Jesus, I want you to be the center of my life. Fill me now with your Holy Spirit and empower me to kingdom living. As I dedicate myself to completing these meditations, please help me make a prayer corner in my home where I can spend time with you each day. Amen.

17

Why, God, Why?

For the prayer corner:
A question mark cut out of construction paper.

O Lord, how long shall I cry for help, and you will not listen?
Or cry to you, "Violence!" and you will not save?
Why do you make me see wrong-doing and look at trouble?
Destruction and violence are before me;
strife and contention arise. (Habakkuk 1:2-3)

I am reminded of Jane, who called the Christian Parents Help Line for Sexual Abuse. She thought her neighborhood was safe from "those kind of people." The sad truth is that a child molester can be a person you invite into your home. Jane discovered this when her son was molested last summer by the "nice" teenage boy who baby-sat her child. The authorities were contacted and Jane's son started counseling with a sexual abuse therapist.

Jane and her husband are trying to put the past behind them. Sundays they go to church, and Jane has kept the language of a Christian. From behind this controlled and reserved facade, she dares to reveal her true feelings toward God.

Her voice cracked with anger when she exploded, "All the prayers I said for my son's protection were wasted! My child never did anything to hurt anyone. I taught Sunday school, and we gave a portion of our income every week to our church. Why, oh why, did God let this awful thing happen to our little boy?"

The counselor had several years' experience on the Help Line and gave Jane all the time she needed to verbalize her anger. She didn't judge. Instead, she assured Jane that God was big enough to take any abuse or questions. She also expressed her sympathy, telling Jane she was sorry such a sad thing had happened to her little boy.

Perhaps because Jane could remain anonymous, she brought up a thought which had been troubling her for some time. She asked, almost in a whisper, to the gentle, understanding voice on the telephone, "I really don't believe in an all-loving gentle God anymore like I used to before this happened to my family. When I have so many doubts, I lie awake at night and even wonder sometimes if I am still a Christian."

Jane, like many Christian parents, was experiencing a crisis in her faith at the same time she was having a crisis in her family. When a *bad* thing happened to Jane's child, she thought God was the *bad* person who allowed the *bad* thing to happen to her son. Jane was even wondering if God was getting even with her for some *bad* thing she did a long time ago.

The Christian telephone counselor pointed out that God was simply not in that kind of relationship with us. He does not keep a scoreboard of our wrongs. He is not out there waiting to get even with us. Instead, she reminded Jane, someone she loved had been deeply wounded. Jane was feeling with the emotions God had given her.

Anger is probably one of the first and strongest emotions a parent feels after such a disclosure. Whenever we are angry, we blame someone. We ask questions and say illogical things.

Jane was helped to understand that it may have appeared she was closer to God before the disclosure. The distance between her and God had not changed. Now she was only in a different relationship with God.

Jane protested at first: "But I was a much better Christian before all this happened."

19

The counselor suggested Jane might want to give herself permission to accept the changes in her life without judging everything. Her life had changed greatly after the disclosure and would continue to change as her family moved along in the recovery and healing process. Life was not better or worse now, only different.

Jane, a hurting parent, found comfort when she was reminded that God loved her even when she felt unlovable. He accepted her just the way she was. She finished the phone call by saying, "If God can accept me and all I am feeling, I guess I can accept me too. Maybe it is time to stop asking God why and start asking for his help."

How Does My Faith Measure Up?

- What has happened to your faith since you discovered your child was sexually abused?

- Do you blame God for not protecting your child? Are you angry with God? Tell God your feelings.

Prayer of Faith

O God, I worry sometimes about my faith, if it is big enough or good enough. I'm so glad to know that what is important is not how much faith I have, but how much love you have for me. Amen.

THIRD DAY

A Season of Sorrow

For the prayer corner: A dried-up leaf.

For everything there is a season,
and a time for every matter under heaven. (Ecclesiastes 3:1)

Read Ecclesiastes 3:1-8.

When I discovered my child had been abused by an adult she knew and trusted, I was in a state of shock. I went to the library to get material on sexual abuse, came directly home, closed the door of my bedroom, and began reading. The more I read, the worse I felt. The life energy drained out of me. For three days I lay on my bed, helpless and heartbroken. Where are the words to express the pain and horror that immobilized me? Even today, seven years later, I have trouble finding words to describe the gamut of emotions I felt. Few things are more difficult or sadder than for a parent to stand beside an innocent child who has become a victim of sexual abuse.

My husband was the only person I talked to about what happened. Like most parents, we did not seek professional help for our child until considerable time had passed. *Maybe* it was just too painful. *Maybe* we had trouble getting used to the idea. *Maybe* we were just too scared to turn our child over to a stranger, inexperienced in counseling sexual abuse survivors. What I do know happened was that I carried a large burden of sadness for a long time. No one knew it except my husband, who saw my shining eyes turn to pools of tears at the mention of our child's past.

If I hadn't found Norman Vincent Peale's book *Inspiring Messages for Daily Living*,[1] I don't think it would have been possible for me to come out of my season of sorrow believing in Jesus' care for me. Between the covers of that book, I found a friend who encouraged me without even knowing my name. A friend who supplied me with Scripture verses that gave me hope and strength. A friend who offered me prayer tips on how to seek the Lord in my darkest moments.

I had never been aware of such a need in my life, and now I learned that the Bible could actually be my greatest helper. I referred again and again to the forty life-changing Scriptures for comfort and encouragement. It took about a year for me to believe God was capable of helping my child and our family's special need.

I followed one suggestion in the book at a time. The first and most powerful suggestion was "practice the presence." I began to believe that always, at any hour of the day or night, in whatever circumstance or condition, Jesus Christ was actually present. After all, he promised "I am with you always" (Matthew 28:20). I shared my sorrow with Christ in a simple place. Every Monday morning when I swept my front porch and carport, I unburdened myself to God and believed that he would relieve and assist me. To this day my favorite prayer time is when I am outside, surrounded by the beautiful world God created.

In Ecclesiastes I am reminded of how many different passages of time and seasons we pass through in a lifetime. The time to laugh is different from the time to weep. I won't say it is easy to recover after parents discover the sad truth their child has become a victim of sexual abuse. I will say it *is* possible to pass from one season of sadness to the next season in life.

God does not cause or bring sadness into our lives. Sorrow is a part of the human experience. When sorrow comes, give yourself permission to express it in any way you choose. Lastly, remember God's word tells us there is a time for every season. There will be another season soon.

A Time for Everything

For everything there is a season, and a time for every matter under heaven:

a time to be born, and a time to die;
a time to plant, and a time to pluck up what is planted;
a time to kill, and a time to heal;
a time to break down, and a time to build up;
a time to weep, and a time to laugh;
a time to mourn, and a time to dance;
a time to throw away stones, and a time to gather stones together;
a time to embrace, and a time to refrain from embracing;
a time to seek, and a time to lose;
a time to keep, and a time to throw away;
a time to tear, and a time to sew;
a time to keep silence, and a time to speak;
a time to love, and a time to hate;
a time for war, and a time for peace. (Ecclesiastes 3:1-8)

For Reflection

- What does this Scripture say to you?

- What is one way you can lighten your burden of sorrow?

- Is there a pastor or someone you can trust with whom to talk about your sorrow?

Prayer of Sorrow

O God, every tree tells me there are seasons in the world. You have made people to have seasons as well. There is a season in me of great sorrow. Help me to get to know you better, Lord, so you can share my sadness. Amen.

23

FOURTH DAY

Losing Your Temper

For the prayer corner:
A rock and a small stick glued to a paper heart.

*So Moses took the staff from before the Lord, as he had com-
manded him. Moses and Aaron gathered the assembly together
before the rock, and he said to them, "Listen, you rebels, shall we
bring water for you out of this rock?" Then Moses lifted up his
hand and struck the rock twice with his staff; water came out
abundantly, and the congregation and their livestock drank.*

(Numbers 20:9-11)

Read Numbers 20:1-13.

Imagine for a moment the responsibility that lay on the shoulders of Moses as he led the children of Israel out of Egypt. He was
like a parent to these hurting people who had been mistreated
physically and emotionally. The beginning of their journey out of
bondage is riddled with accounts of grumbling and complaints
against Moses and the Lord. All Moses could offer the Israelites
was his continued trust in the Almighty God.

24

Moses started out doing the right thing. He went to the tent of meeting and prayed about the problems he was facing. The Lord was eager to show his presence to his children. He spoke to Moses and told him to take the staff and gather the people together before a rock. He said Moses would only have to speak to that rock and it would pour out water for the people and their livestock.

As Moses faced the grumbling people, his temper got in the way. He did not follow the instructions of the Lord. Instead, he first blasted the Israelites: "Listen you rebels, must we bring you water out of this rock?" Then he blasted the rock with his staff.

Moses, like any person who is called to be strong for the weak, was tired of the whole affair. He was tired of the people, tired of the problems, and tired of the complaints.

As a parent of a sexually abused child, I relate to Moses. I get tired of the pain of remembering the things that were done to my child against her wishes. I get tired of the behaviors my child acts out because of the hurts she carries. Like Moses, I lose my temper with those closest to me.

One of the hardest struggles I came to grips with was my temper. As a Christian parent, I started with good intentions. I sought the Lord with my parenting problems. I asked for guidance. I even heard his voice in my spiritual ears telling me to stop or be still. Instead of pulling back and cooling down, I chose to stay in the alarm position. I was always ready to react instead of respond to the needs of the members of my own family. I hurt myself and others with the angry outbursts or silent walls I put up in my home.

After my temper tantrums, I felt awful about myself and my behavior. I felt that one part of me was unclean and unlovable. I was convinced God couldn't love me when I was an awful parent.

One day three words changed my attitude toward myself and my temper. I did an act of kindness for a stranger. She looked into my eyes and said, " God loves you." The words sounded trite at first. I was tempted to forget her comment immediately. But I started to wonder if the words were spoken by the Lord for me. Maybe they were words that could heal me. I let the meaning behind the words sink into me like rock-spring water on parched ground.

"God loves me"—period! I can't even change God's love for me when my behavior changes because God's love for me stays the same. God loves me when I can control my temper, and he loves me when I lose control of my temper. When I am weak, and when I fall below my calling of being the Christian parent I desire to be, my God still loves me.

What Does My Face Reveal?

- A checklist for your current behavior with your family:

[ ] Unkindness	[ ] Understanding
[ ] Hatred	[ ] Gentleness
[ ] Harshness	[ ] Patient
[ ] Impatience	[ ] Cheerfulness
[ ] Rejection	[ ] Peaceful
[ ] Blame	[ ] Compassion

- God desires each one of his children to find peace and harmony despite our circumstances and problems. List two ways you can control your temper and bring peace to yourself, your child, and your family.

Temper Prayer

O God, please help me control my temper. I sometimes don't realize when I let my temper get out of control. I have hurt others and myself. Help me to seek forgiveness from anyone I have hurt because I have let my temper control me. Please be the Lord of my temper. Amen.

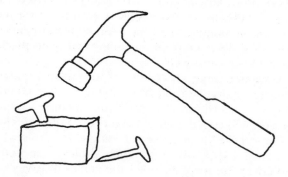

FIFTH DAY

Hurting Each Other

For the prayer corner:
A hammer and a piece of wood with a nail pounded in it.

*Then Jesus gave a loud cry and breathed his last. And the curtain
of the temple was torn in two, from top to bottom. Now when the
centurion, who stood facing him, saw that in this way he
breathed his last, he said, "Truly this man was God's Son!"*

(Mark 15:37-39)

When Jesus died, a great rumbling sounded and the earth began
to quake as darkness covered the hill. The centurion spoke with
conviction. A great misfortune had been done to Jesus, the Son of
God.

Are we not like the centurion standing on Calvary, so caught up
in the events of the day that we also miss the reality of Jesus?
When a Christian parent is caught in the middle of a wounded
family, it is easier to stand away from the cross than at the foot of
it.

For Anne, a single mother of two years, life was anything but
normal since she and her husband, Tony, divorced. She reentered

the work force, and her three latchkey sons were on their own. When Anne discovered her middle son, James, was spending too much time playing video games with the man next door, it was too late. She discovered the neighbor had been playing sexual games with her son as well.

Anne wanted some advice but was too embarrassed to call anyone in her family. She thought maybe her pastor could help. He expressed concern for all of the family members, especially for James. He encouraged Anne to contact the authorities immediately and report the incident. Next, he advised her to read her insurance benefits to know how much professional counseling it would cover. He recommended the names of two sexual abuse therapists. Then he scheduled an appointment to see her Saturday morning.

When Anne met with her pastor, he had a hammer, a piece of wood, and nails on his desk. Picking up the hammer he held it in his hand and said, "Anne, you have the right to feel angry or hateful toward the person who hurt your child. But remember, sometimes angry feelings get displaced and a parent can take their anger out on an innocent child. Remember your words and actions are like a hammer. They can pound in hurts and wound your family, or your words and actions can build strength and hope for your family through Christ."

He reminded her of the call to be a Christian parent even in difficult times. "We have a definite job similar to those of nails," he said. "We join the individual members of our family, or boards, together. We are also a burden-bearer, much as a nail supports what is hung on it. That is not an easy task for any parent."

Anne bowed her head. Tears fell on her blue cotton dress. The pastor passed the tissue box. As Anne blew her nose, she asked, "How can I ever be that kind of parent after this has happened? You don't know how much rage I feel or the awful things I said to my son."

Leaning forward in his chair, the pastor replied, "Your family is under a tremendous amount of pressure right now. That pressure is going to be on for quite some time. It would be better for your child if you did not explode under the pressure, if at all possible. Instead of hurting each other, why don't you come in and talk with me about your angry feelings?"

Anne agreed with the pastor. Her child was hurt enough. She'd try to do her best not to bring any more pain into his life. What her son needed most right now was a loving and supportive parent. While that might be difficult, it would not be impossible. She went home to try.

I Drive Nails

- Place on the floor a piece of wood in which nails have already been pounded in. As you say each petition, hit the piece of wood with the hammer. Or you may pray the confession to God by kneeling on the floor and holding several different size nails in your hand.

- I drive nails when I think that suffering only takes place far away from me in places like India or Africa, and not within my very own family.

- I drive nails when I destroy a person's reputation by revealing those secrets I know, those weaknesses I suspect.

- I drive nails into myself when days go by without a prayer.

- I drive nails when I see the walls my child puts up and I back away.

- I drive nails when I do not choose to make peace.

- A period of private prayer in total silence, followed by:

Prayer of Sorrow

O my God, I am sorry that I have sinned. Please forgive me. I know you love me and want to help me live out your example. Amen.

SIXTH DAY

Springs of Bitterness

For the prayer corner:
A popsicle stick or small piece of lumber.

Then Moses ordered Israel to set out from the Red Sea, and they went into the wilderness of Shur. They went three days in the wilderness and found no water. When they came to Marah, they could not drink the water of Marah because it was bitter. That is why it was called Marah. And the people complained against Moses, saying, "What shall we drink?" He cried out to the Lord; and the Lord showed him a piece of wood; he threw it into the water, and the water became sweet. (Exodus 15:22-25)

The Israelites had finally been released from the stronghold of the Egyptians. When they made camp the first night, they sang praises to the Lord for miraculously opening the Red Sea. They were confident the Lord would lead them to the Promised Land. However, three days later the Israelites—tired and thirsty from wandering in the desert—began to question whether the Lord still watched over them. The bitter water the Lord supplied in the desert was a symbol to the people of their own bitterness.

Bitterness and resentment are two problems a parent must face after an incest disclosure, perhaps because most children are sexually abused by a person they know and trust. Often the abuse takes place in their own home.

Melody was a parent drinking the bitter water of resentment since sexual abuse caused havoc on her home front. She had chosen her second husband with care. Jack—a manager at a large manufacturing firm—seemed to enjoy spending time with eleven-year-old Amy. After a two-year courtship, he and Melody were married and moved into Jack's suburban home. At Jack's urging, Melody enrolled in an evening college class one night a week. He offered to take care of Amy. Later, she found out how he was taking care of her daughter.

One evening Melody's class was canceled and she arrived home earlier than expected. She found her husband in bed with her daughter. Without a moment's hesitation, she called 911 and pressed charges against her husband.

Rebuilding their lives has not been easy. Three years later Melody cannot even say the name *Jack* without bitterness. She continues to struggle with resentment toward her daughter for not telling her what Jack was doing when she was at night school.

Melody does not often think much about God because she is spending much of her daily energy regretting the past. She blames herself for trusting Jack with her daughter. Melody does not intend to see a counselor because she is convinced counselors are as messed up as she. No, she will wing it alone. But the problem remains: Melody is a wounded bird with a broken wing and a broken heart that time will not mend. Only one medicine can heal her pain.

Just as Moses was instructed to throw the wood into the bitter water to make the water sweet, Melody must throw the weight (or wood) of bitterness out of her life. That doesn't mean she will never feel angry toward Jack again. Of course she will, but that anger is no longer controlling her present actions or limiting the quality of life she shares with her daughter Amy.

How can she release her bitterness when such an act of violence has been committed against her daughter? The fact is that neither Melody nor any other parents of a sexually abused child can ever come to a place of peace or reconciliation with the past *until he or she is ready to*. When the time is right, a parent will still only be able to exchange the bitter water for the sweet with God's help.

Pulling Up the Roots of Bitterness

- Check the person or persons you feel resentful toward:

[ ] Police	[ ] Relatives
[ ] Counselors	[ ] Friends
[ ] Sex offender	[ ] Lawyers
[ ] Pastor	[ ] Judges
[ ] Parent	[ ] Jury
[ ] Victim	[ ] God

- How is the resentment you feel effecting your physical, emotional, and spiritual life?

- Pick one person on your list and write one action you can take toward making peace with the past.

Prayer for Strength

O God, I pray for the strength to make changes in my life. I pray for the strength to face the bitterness I carry hidden in my heart. Lord, please cleanse me of a secret sin. Amen.

Healing
the Hurting
Parent

May those who sow in tears reap with shouts of joy.
Those who go out weeping, bearing the seed for sowing,
shall come home with shouts of joy, carrying their sheaves.
—Psalm 126:5-6

SEVENTH DAY

New Beginnings

For the prayer corner:
A pair of sunglasses for a child or an adult.

As he walked along, he saw a man blind from birth. His disciples asked him, "Rabbi, who sinned, this man or his parents, that he was born blind?" Jesus answered, "Neither this man nor his parents sinned." (John 9:1-2)

Read John 9:1-34.

Whenever a tragedy occurs, people ask the same question the disciples asked the Rabbi 2,000 years ago, "Whose fault is this?" When persons are tragically the victims of rape, far too often they are punished unjustly for the sin of sexual violence committed against them, and against their will.

In all cases of sexual abuse, the blame needs to fall not on the victim but on the sex offender who violated the rights of the child and broke the child protection laws. Sexual abuse is *never* a child's fault. Often it is an uncontrollable choice by a sex offender. Until society believes this, parents will struggle as they fight for the legal rights of the survivors of sexual abuse.

Rita's parents were scared when their fifteen-year-old daughter came home with a tear-streaked face and a torn blouse. After calming her down, Rita told them as much as she could. She went to her girlfriend's house after the varsity football game for pizza. Her friend's older brother was visiting from college and had brought a buddy home for the weekend. That buddy offered to walk Rita the six blocks home. It was the visitor, the friend, who did IT to her in the bushes and IT was awful.

Her father wanted to get his gun and give the kid a taste of his own medicine. Instead, her mother persuaded him to call the police. They arrested the clean-cut twenty-two-year-old college student. The family believed that a police report and court date would take back the night of terror their daughter remembers vividly to this day.

Instead, their daughter was like the blind man who had to justify to the Pharisees every action that led up to the night of the rape. The burden of proof fell on the victim and her parents to prove Rita was not a girl who was "asking for it." The lawyer for the defense hurled insult after insult against the quiet Christian girl. It was no different from the Pharisees who insisted on insulting the blind man after his encounter with spit and mud. The only difference was that the blind man was touched in love, and Rita had been touched in violence.

This Scripture passage became the foundation the family used to overcome the ignorance they faced as they proceeded to fight for the rights of their daughter the sexual abuse victim. The media was blind to the grief these parents felt. They mourned their daughter's virginity which was taken in an aggressive and frightening manner.

The wheels of justice grind slowly, and their enthusiasm to see justice done was blinded by the legal process and the trial entrapments. They considered dropping the case because it was postponed twice by the judge. Their lawyer suggested they contact a local support group for rape survivors to find advocates who would encourage them to keep their case open.

When Rita's parents realized they would just have to get into the dirt and mud of life and use good old-fashioned spit and hard work to overcome evil with good, they began to notice a change in attitude. The future looked brighter. They were hopeful about the outcome of the trial.

Whose Fault Is It?

- Whom do you blame for the sexual abuse done to your child?

SOCIETY
[ ] Pornography
[ ] Heavy metal music
[ ] Television

PARENT
[ ] Lack of supervision
[ ] Neglect of child
[ ] Ignorance
[ ] Didn't verify references
[ ] In denial

VICTIM
[ ] Seductive behavior
[ ] Starved for affection
[ ] Seduced the adult
[ ] Ignorance
[ ] Developmentally delayed

- Sexual abuse should not be blamed on society, the parents, or the victim. Responsibility for the act lies with the offender and not with the child.

Prayer for Wisdom

Lord, help me to recognize where responsibility lodges and not to play the blame game. Let me see your healing, saving, and righting works. Amen.

EIGHTH DAY

Food in the Desert

For the prayer corner:
A glass of water and a slice of bread.

You in your great mercies did not forsake them in the wilderness;
the pillar of cloud that led them in the way did not leave them by
day, nor the pillar of fire by night that gave light on the way by
which they should go. You gave them your good spirit to instruct
them, and did not withhold your manna from their mouths, and
gave them water for their thirst. Forty years you sustained them
in the wilderness so that they lacked nothing.

(Nehemiah 9:19-21)

A few years after our child's disclosure, the reality of living with
a sexually abused child and trying to parent our wounded child
was extremely difficult. There was no Christian material on sexual
abuse and how the family could deal with it. The parent's guides
weren't even written yet. As far as I was concerned, sexual abuse
was only being addressed from the theoretical viewpoint. I realized I was an Israelite traveling across a dry and barren desert. Just
as God helped Moses to lead the way for the wandering Israelites,

he put people in my path to help me and my family in this difficult time.

I continued to go to church and listen to my pastor preach about God who could change our lives and help families. My pastor was pointing the way to the Promised Land from the other side, and I couldn't find out how to get there. My spiritual life that was once green and lush began to dry up. Most of the time I felt numb from hunger and thirst. I longed to again be filled with inner peace. Other times I felt angry and scared that I could live in this barren wasteland for years.

Then the Lord provided me with a real Moses, a person who had walked in the desert and knew the path to the Promised Land. Surprisingly, this Moses was a woman. She told me to go to the desert.

"You want me to go to the desert?" I questioned. "You've got to be kidding. If you are suggesting I go away, at least I'd like to go to someplace beautiful like Hawaii."

"No," she said. "I am suggesting you go to The Desert House of Prayer. It is a place of silence and renewal. A private room and three meals a day costs twelve dollars. There is a chapel on the grounds, and if you want to talk to someone, there is always a person on staff to listen. I go once a year."

I will never forget the day my family drove up the gravel drive in the middle of the Saguaro National Park near Tucson. The sign read, "No hunting here, except for inner peace." I silently wondered if I could ever find peace and wholeness again.

My sparsely furnished room was like a shedding of my need to take care of anyone except me. I hugged and kissed my husband and children good-bye, closed the door to my room, and slept for three days.

I awoke refreshed. The desert became a place of beauty. The Saguaro cactus were in bloom. Their pink blossoms brought color to the repetitive greens and browns. Coyote pups called out to the night sky as lightning flashed across August skies. Beauty and life abounded. I spent three weeks at the retreat house. In the silence my spiritual ears opened to hear the soft voice of the Lord calling me to be his child again.

I renewed my primary relationship to God and decided to rely on his goodness in my emotional desert. He was just going to have to take care of me, his littlest and neediest child. He didn't send a pillar of cloud or fire as a sign of his presence to me. He sent other signs to remind me of his guidance and direction. On my writing table I set out a piece of bread and a glass of water. For my morning devotion I read Nehemiah 9:19-21. In silence I ate my bread and water as a scriptural prayer thanking God for his nearness and comfort to me.

The Water and the Bread

- Is your spiritual life dry and lifeless Monday through Saturday?
- Do you feed your spiritual body daily? Why or why not?
- What grace do you need most from God today?

Prayer in the Desert

To the thirsty God brings the water of life which is prayer.
To the hungry he brings the bread of life which is his Word.

Ordinary food feeds my body. O God, feed my spiritual body.
Ordinary food helps me grow. O God, help me grow in my faith
and trust.
Ordinary food makes me strong. O God, I am so weak, you are
my strength.
Ordinary food satisfies my hunger. O God, I hunger for you.
Ordinary food keeps me healthy. O God, heal my wounded spirit.
Amen.

NINTH DAY
Assistance Along the Way

For the prayer corner:
A bundle—a small bag stuffed with cotton and tied.

As they went out, they came upon a man from Cyrene named Simon; they compelled this man to carry his cross.

(Matthew 27:32)

As the crowd followed Jesus to Golgotha (the place of the skull), a traveler named Simon was forced to help carry the cross. All Simon did was pick up the wooden cross, rest it on his shoulder, and drag it down the street until he was told to give it back to Jesus. It is not recorded how long he walked with the cross along the Via Dolorosa. In fact, he is never mentioned in Scripture again. What is more revealing is that Jesus, the Son of God, was forced to accept assistance from a stranger to finish his purpose and task. In doing so, Jesus left us with an example of how we can find strength to complete difficult tasks in our lives.

Presently, Survivors of Sexual Abuse support groups for victims and their relatives are being formed in every major city in America. These groups offer parents the chance to listen to other sur-

41

vivors' stories and to tell their own. One parent remarked, "Just being in a room with another parent going through the same things we were, made our pain a little more bearable."

In a support group, you, as a parent can go and have your burdens, worries, and fears lifted for awhile. When you first arrive, a Simon will assist you. Later, as you become stronger, you will be the Simon for the next parent who walks through the door.

The Bible says, "Call to me and I will answer you, and will tell you great and hidden things that you have not known" (Jeremiah 33:3). Many hurting parents find assistance through their telephone. At first my friend was afraid to call the Christian television prayer partner. She worried about what the person would think of her. Then she thought about the person being Simon from Cyrene in the Scripture. Now she begins her call with a silent prayer saying, "Lord, help this person be my Simon."

Most parents think they are able to handle alone the burden of a child who has been molested. In other words, counseling is not an option, but a last resort. This is a serious mistake. The mistake begins with the letter *P* for pride. It was my pride and only my pride that stood in the way of reaching for the professional assistance my child needed to move along in her stages of recovery. By the time I was able to accept the fact that an outsider could assist my child, many valuable years had passed.

I had to come before the Lord and ask his forgiveness for my selfish pride which stood in the way of getting the help our family needed. The wonderful thing about Jesus is that he erases our errors as if they never occurred. He showed me through the Scripture passage on Simon that by my act of obedience, I had become the living word. I had become Simon for my child.

After the initial counseling, I recognized my child was going to have times in her adolescence and adult life that could be confusing and stressful. I wanted to help her as much as I could but realized she might not be able to share some of her feelings with me. Since I wanted her to have the benefit of having an adult friend she could turn to for support, I began to pray for a Simon for my child.

Sometime later I approached a girlfriend who was watching her children leave the nest and asked her if she would consider being an adopted aunt for my daughter. She was flattered and excited at the invitation. I explained the kind of aunt my daughter needed—positive woman role model, a listening ear, and a tenderness toward a girl who had some sad things happen to her in the past.

It has been the best trade-off for both of them. My friend has gotten a second chance to be important in the life of a child. And my daughter now has an adult person who invites her to do fun things. She is also learning she can trust and confide her feelings to her aunt. God has blessed us with many Simons.

Finding the Help You Need

• Counseling: You may have reached the point of wondering if your family should see a counselor. These questions will help you make that determination. If you are still in doubt, your pastor might help you decide. If he does not have training and expertise in this area, he may refer you to a sexual abuse therapist.

• Do you deal with the same issues over and over again without making any perceivable progress? If so, list them.

• Have you reached the point where you cannot talk about the problems without losing emotional control? Or have you stopped talking about the problems? Explain:

• Do you think the problems are affecting other areas of your marriage, family, and life? Does there seem to be no solution?

• Particularly among Christians, counseling can be a sensitive issue. To seek counseling is sometimes seen as an admission of fault or failure. However, counseling often is an aid to solving a problem. And the problem here is communication. Because it is so difficult to talk about these issues with others, counseling can be the aid you need to deal with post-sexual-abuse syndrome. By seeking counseling you demonstrate your readiness to work for solutions. This is a strength, not a weakness.

Prayer for Assistance

• In silence take a moment to ask the Lord to help you find the people you need to assist your family.

TENTH DAY
Finding Peace in the Storm

For the prayer corner:
The words *Peace! Be still!* written on a piece of paper.

But he was in the stern, asleep on the cushion; and they woke him up and said to him, "Teacher, do you not care that we are perishing?"
He woke up and rebuked the wind, and said to the sea, "Peace! Be still!" Then the wind ceased, and there was a dead calm.

(Mark 4:38-39)

Read Mark 4:35-41.

John Paul grew up in a small fishing village, and he spent every waking hour near the water. Skipping stones off the shoreline, he dreamed of Alaskan waters and of sighting blue whales off schooner ships. Instead of going to college, he went to Alaska and landed a job on a fishing boat. His first time out, John Paul discovered even the most weathered seamen with their scientific instruments could not conquer the unpredictable ocean with its fury. John Paul didn't have a seaman's stomach, however, and he bought a plane ticket back to the placid waters of the harbor. He reunited with his high school sweetheart. They married, and children soon followed. John Paul wanted his boys to have the freedom he had growing up. Never once did he consider the boys could be in danger. After all, John Paul knew every street, cranny, and neighbor in his boyhood town.

Disaster struck as it does to so many unknowing and trusting parents. Their youngest son was befriended by a man who rented a house just two blocks from their home. Puppies were the bait used to trap the unsuspecting boy, and he was molested by the stranger for one summer. That fall the stranger mysteriously moved away, never to be seen or heard from again.

John Paul became the storm. Everywhere he walked, waves of guilt tossed him here and there. His eyes blazed like lightning when he thought of his child being violated by a man several times his son's size. His hot curse words cracked like thunder in a darkened purple sky. Every gust of wind John Paul blew in anger and frustration only increased the intensity of the storm within him.

John Paul's family was almost shipwrecked. Each parent silently blamed the other. The family was ripping apart at the helm. The boat was ready to shatter into pieces and leave the family to drown. No one had a life jacket. If fact, none of the other children knew why Daddy was so angry.

I'd like to tell you that one day John Paul said, "Hey, God, somebody said you can calm the storm in me. The Bible says all I have to say is 'Peace! Be still!' How about it, God, will you do it?"

I'm sorry to say that didn't happen to John Paul. I don't think that happens to most parents who are expressing a variety of emotions after they discover their child has been abused. Storms have been known to rage on for weeks or months or years. The sad truth is, some parents and families never recover.

In stormy times, it is easy to think Jesus doesn't care about the awful things that happen to us, and we can feel abandoned. Although Jesus was sleeping, he was still in the boat with the disciples. He was in the storm. That means Jesus is in the middle of your worst storm.

The Lord never gave up hope for John Paul. One day in the smallest of ways the Lord revealed to him that the emotional abuse he was inflicting on his family was as offensive as the sexual abuse inflicted on his child. John Paul didn't know Jesus well enough to wake him up and plead with him to stop the storm. Instead, he desperately cried out, "Help me, God! I'm drowning!" The Lord's merciful hand reached down and rescued John Paul, who has never been the same.

Am I an Instrument of God's Peace?

- Peace is a journey that begins with a single step. As you answer the questions yes or no, you will know how far you have walked on the peace march against sexual violence of innocent children.
  - Do I believe in peaceful resolutions and nonviolence?
    [ ] Yes [ ] No
  - Is peacemaking a conscious decision I make each day?
    [ ] Yes [ ] No
  - Do I live and speak the message of peace to others?
    [ ] Yes [ ] No
  - Do I desire to work for peace, even in adverse circumstances? [ ] Yes [ ] No
  - Do I want to seek for the peace of the place where I live?
    [ ] Yes [ ] No
  - Do I believe God's Word gives peace in all circumstances?
    [ ] Yes [ ] No
  - Do I spend time with the Prince of Peace daily?
    [ ] Yes [ ] No
  - Do I pray for peace daily? [ ] Yes [ ] No

Prayer for Peace

O God, let there be peace on earth and let it begin with me. Amen.

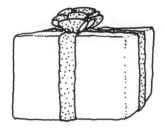

ELEVENTH DAY

The Gift of Forgiveness

For the prayer corner: A small empty box wrapped as a gift.

Blessed rather are those who hear the word of God and obey it!
(Luke 11:28)

Pastor Josh briskly walked across the five-acre campus to the parsonage. His family was ready to leave for summer Bible camp in the mountains. Pastor Josh was proud of his successful ten-year ministry. Others envied him. Life not only had been good to him, it had been fantastic. That was until tragedy struck, unexpectedly.

On the last day of camp, Josh and his son went to their cabin to change for chapel. It was then that Josh noticed how swollen his son's genitals were. "Did you get bitten by a bug or hurt yourself?" he asked his son. Michael turned to hide his front side, exposing his back to his father. A red swollen anus shocked Josh. He questioned his son further. The evasive answers disturbed him.

Finally, after considerable effort, some bribes, and a lot of persuasion, Michael reluctantly gave his father the name of the man who gave him money to buy candy from the canteen. To Josh's horror, the boy named a deacon in his church. It didn't seem possible, but it was obvious now that *someone* had sexually abused their child. From the story their son gave them, it could well have been the deacon.

Pastor Josh could not believe that a deacon in his church was responsible for what he discovered. He considered facing the man, but lacked the courage. While he believed his son, it was only his nine-year-old's word against the deacon's. Suppose the deacon denied it?

He wrestled with the idea of taking the problem to his board, but the thought of possible public exposure for his successful and prosperous church stopped him. Instead, he tried to ignore the whole incident, keeping his child from any further contact with the deacon. What Pastor Josh had counseled others to do—face their problems—he found difficult to do himself. He soon asked for a transfer to another city, hoping to bury the problem completely. Facing the deacon time after time was just too much for him.

Time passed, and Pastor Josh found his preaching was more and more ineffective. He was being turned inside out with secret sins. They haunted him day and night. Often he woke up in a cold sweat, repeating the same words over and over. "You want seventy times seventy, God? Never! I'll never forgive that man. I hate him for what he did to my son. I hate him for making me leave the largest congregation I ever had. I hate him! I hate him! I hate him!"

The festering hate and unforgiveness had just about broken the pastor's back when the Holy Spirit intervened. A roommate from seminary wrote and told Josh he would lead a week-long retreat for pastors to address their total needs: physical, emotional, and spiritual. His friend promised a restful setting on a steel blue lake in the mountains, and a chance for them to renew an old friendship.

Josh welcomed the invitation but failed to realize that once he arrived at the camp, the mountains, cabins, and canteen would flood his memories of the past. One evening late into the retreat, the broken pastor revealed to his friend the festering sins hindering his ministry and his relationship with his family. He confessed that his child had been molested by a deacon in his church ten years before. He cried the years of tears he had held back for so long—unforgiving tears of hate, bitter gasps of unforgiveness, and the pride that allowed him to bury the problem.

The retreat pastor's words were just what Josh needed. "There is forgiveness for us too, Josh. Pastors need it as much as lay people. Forgiveness is a gift you give to yourself and the child molester again and again. Why don't you give God all the hate, all the tears of recrimination, and the false pride that has kept you from being the instrument of peace God intended you to be?"

At the closing burning service the next night, Josh committed all the sins to the crimson and orange flames.

Before they parted, his friend reminded Josh that counseling was an important part of the healing process which his son needed. "There are other pastors whose children were abused by trusted church workers," he told him. "We have qualified sexual abuse therapists, and support groups in every city I travel to. I will send you the list when I return home. Our denomination also has a packet of resources you will find helpful which I will include."

Josh received the information on sexual abuse the pastor promised, along with a small wrapped gift. When Josh lifted the cover on the box, he found it empty except for a card that read, "Accepting forgiveness is a gift we give ourselves. Giving forgiveness is a gift we give to others. God's forgiveness is his gift to us which sets our spirit free."

An Offering of Forgiveness

- Plan a time and a place where you will not be interrupted when you make your offering to yourself. Spending some time in silence will prepare you for the healing to take place. When you are ready, say these words:

- I was (angry, scared, in denial, overwhelmed, shocked, paralyzed with guilt, etc.) when I discovered (child's name) was a sexually abused child. I forgive myself for any words I said out of (denial, fear, thoughtlessness, etc.). I forgive myself for my (bitterness, ill thoughts, unforgiveness, unforgiving hate, etc.) that kept me from dealing with the problem. I forgive myself for (not believing, protecting, defending, or coming to the aid) of my child. I forgive myself for the lack of courage that kept me from facing the child molester.

Prayer for Forgiveness

O God, I accept your gift of forgiveness to me, and I claim your comfort, your peace, and your love. Amen.

- Write what you are feeling now.

The Hurting Child

Let the little children come to me, and do not stop them;
for it is to such as these that the kingdom of God belongs.
—Luke 18:16

TWELFTH DAY

Hiding from the Truth

For the prayer corner: An apple and a bowl of dirt.

Now the serpent was more crafty than any other wild animal
that the Lord God had made. He said to the woman, "Did God
say, 'You shall not eat from any tree in the garden'?"

The woman said to the serpent, "We may eat of the fruit of the
trees in the garden; but God said, 'You shall not eat of the fruit of
the tree that is in the middle of the garden, nor shall you touch it,
or you shall die.' "

But the serpent said to the woman, "You will not die; for God
knows that when you eat of it your eyes will be opened, and you
will be like God, knowing good and evil." (Genesis 3:1-5)

Read Genesis 3:1-24.

A crafty snake tricked Eve and convinced her that if she ate the
fruit, it would make her wise. She took a bite of fruit and offered
some to Adam. Immediately they realized they had done wrong.
At first they were ashamed, then they became afraid. They hid
themselves from the Lord God, walking in the garden.

Soon they heard God calling, "Adam, have you eaten some fruit from the tree of which I told you not to eat?" Adam answered by putting the blame on Eve. Eve was able to tell God she was tricked and who tricked her. God in his parental wisdom put blame on the crafty serpent. Although Adam and Eve were deceived by the serpent and stumbled into sin, as adults they had to face consequences for disobeying God. Yet God in mercy clothed them, made life tolerable for them, and continued relating with them.

Children who have been molested are tricked by shrewd adults who use children's bodies for their own selfish desires. Often a child molester will threaten children with physical harm if they tell anyone the secret. Children are afraid to tell, even their parents. They hide the molestation from everyone. This stretches into many years of denial, sometimes to themselves and sometimes to others. They feel that if anyone knew what happened to them, they wouldn't be liked or respected. How sad! They are carrying a burden of guilt that does not belong to them.

Bobby went to baseball camp, and when he returned, he was no longer interested in playing on the team. His mother questioned him several times, and the answer was always the same, "Aw, Mom, nothing happened. I just don't like baseball anymore."

Six months later Julia received a telephone call from another concerned mother. She told Julia that the coach had taken Bobby and her son for a hike in the woods where they showed each other their private parts. Julia was furious at Bobby for not telling her the truth about what happened. By the time he returned from school that afternoon, she was a raving maniac. She said and did things she still regrets to this day. Her words have hung heavy in the air for years.

The apple in the prayer corner is a reminder of how human it is for all of us to withhold information, especially when we are scared or ashamed. In the story of Adam and Eve, God never stopped caring or loving the human beings he had made. Instead, he accepted their weakness. No matter how many years have passed, children who have been molested need to be told they are loved the same or perhaps more for the courage they showed in telling their secret.

The bowl of dirt in the prayer corner reminds us parents that we are only human. Adam's body wasn't made out of some heavenly mixture, and neither are ours. The Lord remembers that we are made from dust (Psalm 103:14). There are no professional schools for parents of sexually abused children. We have all made mistakes and have failed from time to time in being the Christian parents we want to be. Only with God's great grace can we turn these mistakes into opportunities for growth. The only true failure comes when we stop trying. Place your hands in the bowl of dirt and feel the touch of your humanness. Be aware of the presence of the Lord in your prayer corner.

* * *

Can I Tell You My Secret?

Dear Mom and Dad,

I have been wanting to talk to you about something bad that happened to me. Well, I don't know if it's bad or not, but I have to tell you. You see, when I lived in El Salvador, my uncle used to touch me in places I didn't want to be touched. I didn't know what to do, or what to say. I thought that if I told him not to do it he would get mad at me and hit me or something. It has taken me a while to get the courage to come and tell you, but now that I've told you, I feel a little better.

  Love,
  Marisol

Dear Marisol,

We think your idea of writing a letter to us is a good one. Sometimes we may seem too busy to listen to the things you want to tell us, but we don't mean to be. Did you know when your dad and I were children we kept secrets? Things like where our secret hiding place was or the secret password to get into our clubhouse.

There are lots of different kinds of secrets. A secret about someone touching your body in a place that makes you feel strange is a private secret. Private secrets are often the most difficult secrets to tell another person. It took a lot of courage for you to tell us you were touched by your uncle in places where you didn't want to be touched. We are very proud of you for coming to us with such a difficult secret to tell.

Of course you didn't know what to do or say when your uncle did things to you because you were so young then. Do you remember how little you were when you lived with your first family? You hadn't even learned how to tie your shoes yet.

It sounds as if you were frightened and worried about getting hit if you disobeyed him. Marisol, anyone would have been scared. Mom would have done the very same thing if she were you.

When you are ready to share more about your secret, we will have some questions to ask you. Questions like, What happened? Or how many times? We care about the things that happened to you before you came to live in our family. We want to know as much as you can remember about your past or as much as you can tell us. Maybe the easiest way you could begin would be to draw some pictures. You could let the pictures tell your story to us.

The most important thing about your secret is to tell all of it. Even the part that makes you feel the worst. Because if you leave any part out, then you still have a secret. Besides, there is no better feeling in the world than to know that your parents love you as always—before they found out about your secret, and after you told them your secret.

There is Someone who knows everyone's secrets, and it doesn't change the way he feels about us. He is God. Aren't you glad you can tell God things you just can't tell anyone else? God is always there to listen and to help you with the things that happened to you in the past.

Love,
Mom and Dad

Dear God:
We all have secrets, but some of us have different secrets. Secrets are not supposed to be told, but I have a secret that I can't keep anymore. It's even pretty hard for me to tell you, God, that my uncle touched me on my private parts. I have so many questions. Every time I think about what happened, I get scared and sick at the same time. God, would you stay close to me when I feel so scared? I am such a little person who had such a big-person experience. God, don't leave me. I need you.
Marisol

* * *

Hiding the Secret

- Who told you that your child was molested?

- Do you recall the first statements (or that of a witness) that sexual abuse had occurred? Please write them.

- If your child did not come to you first with the disclosure, has that affected your relationship with your child?

Prayer for Reality

O God, I hurt, knowing that sex offenders are often friends and family. I don't understand how or why they scheme against vulnerable children. As a parent I am caught in the middle between the pain and the deceit. Forgive me for any actions I have done or things I have said that have brought additional pain and suffering to my child. Amen.

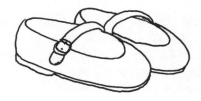

THIRTEENTH DAY
Shame and Humiliation

For the prayer corner: A pair of your child's shoes.

Then the soldiers of the governor took Jesus into the governor's headquarters, and they gathered the whole cohort around him. They stripped him and put a scarlet robe on him, and after twisting some thorns into a crown, they put it on his head. They put a reed in his right hand and knelt before him and mocked him, saying, "Hail, King of the Jews!" They spat on him, and took the reed and struck him on the head. After mocking him, they stripped him of the robe and put his own clothes on him. Then they led him away to crucify him. (Matthew 27:27-31)

One Lenten Sunday my pastor preached a sermon about the ability of Jesus to understand our deepest hurts and private wounds. He didn't address sexual abuse in his sermon, but I began to wonder if it were possible for Jesus to relate to the heartache of sexual abuse? I was uncertain because Jesus' sexuality is not addressed in the Bible. Yet when I studied his suffering on the cross, I realized his clothing was removed against his wishes. My child's clothing was also removed against her wishes. As I meditated on this Scripture, I believed Jesus was capable of feeling my child's personal pain and suffering because he too experienced abuse before he went to the cross. If anyone could understand how my child felt, it would be the Christ.

My spontaneous prayer became a Scripture prayer. When I read these verses, I placed my wounded child in the trust of the Lord's human compassion. Each time I picked up my Bible, I asked the Lord to help me teach my child that Jesus was a person who could understand and help her with any painful memories, even her deepest emotions about the abuse.

As I got in touch with the human qualities of Jesus, I began to look inward at my own human ability to feel my child's pain and sadness. At the beginning, I only wanted my child to tell me the facts about the abuse: What happened? How many times? I hadn't even touched the shadow of my child's feelings about being molested. I never considered how she felt when she was betrayed in an act of violence by a person she trusted. Maybe a part of me didn't want to, for much of the time I was grieving over the loss of my child's innocence.

I knew I needed to change, but I didn't know how, so I placed a pair of my child's shoes in my prayer corner and reflected on these questions. What does betrayal feel like to a seven-year-old? What would I do with my angry feelings? Would I tell my best friend when I felt sad about the abuse? Would I feel ashamed if my friends found out it happened to me? How would I hide my feelings? Would I pretend it never happened?

Answers took time to find because I couldn't relate to the emotional devastation my child was feeling. My problem was that I could feel sad, but not the sadness my child woke up with day after day, year after year. I had nothing so awful in my past that I cringed with shame every time I remembered it. I prayed for God to give me a heart that could feel what my child was feeling.

Slowly I began to watch my body and emotions change. I became more tolerant to the disruptive behaviors my child exhibited. I began to show kindness toward my child by my body movements. I walked more softly around her. When she made a mistake, I didn't always pounce on her like a tiger ready to come in for the kill. The Lord answered my prayer by giving me a compassionate heart toward my child. I was able to speak gentle, considerate, soft-spoken words of encouragement and love.

This opened the door for both of us and gave us the desire to talk to each other. I made up a game, and each day we shared one feeling we had that day. Soon my daughter was looking forward to spending time with me. She was also learning to share some of her feelings about other things not as threatening as the sexual abuse conversations. Later, when she was ready, she started to talk about her feelings and the sad things that had happened to her.

I've learned a valuable lesson: When people are hurting, they need more than an accurate analysis and diagnosis, more than personal advice and assistance. They need to know that someone is always there to listen to their feelings.

* * *

Why Did This Happen to Me?

Dear Mom and Dad,

When I think about what happened to me, sometimes I ask myself, Why did this have to happen to me? I wish I had a different uncle. I wish I could start my life all over again from the very beginning. I know I can't change things now. But I wonder why these things happened to me.

Love,
Marisol

Dear Marisol,

Probably the most difficult thing to understand is why certain things happen to some people and not to others. Sometimes we never get an answer to the question, Why me? But we will try to give you some answers to think about. Children are just too little to know when a person they trust is tricking them. They get tricked because they are told that what they are doing is okay when the older person knows it is not okay. Other times children are forced to do things they don't want to do because threats are made of what would happen if they didn't obey. Maybe they were told they would get hit or loose something they love very much. Older people who want to use children for their own pleasure might even offer candy or gifts in an effort to make children do things with them.

Today more and more people are trying to teach children the difference between good and bad touches. Children are learning that not all people but some people want to harm children. The best way to prevent someone from tricking you is to tell an adult who will listen when you don't feel safe with someone.

When I was little, I wondered why different things happened to some people and not to others. Especially when I saw good things happening, I thought, Why couldn't everybody have the same thing happen to them?

At some time or another we all wish we could start our lives all over again. In that way we could take out all the people and things that hurt us. If I had only one wish in the world, I would wish that your uncle had not let this happen to you. But then I have to agree with you that we can not change the things that have happened to us. There is one bad thing that will never happen to you again. Your uncle can never hurt you or touch you on your private parts again.

You may never find the right answer or an answer good enough to the question, Why did this happen to me? But the most important thing to remember is this: The things that your uncle did to you were not your fault, even if you did not stop the things you were doing. What your uncle did to you was wrong and never should have happened.

Your father and I are so very proud of you. I know it must be very hard to talk about your past, but we are interested in the good and the bad things that happened to you. Thank you for trusting us with your feelings.

Love,
Mom and Dad

Dear God,

I have just so many questions that seem unanswered right now. All I know is that I am glad I can ask my parents some of the things that have been bothering me. They said you understand everything because you are God. Is it possible you can help me understand the things that happened to me?

Marisol

* * *

He Takes Our Wounds

- Has your victimized child been able to share with you some or all of the sexual things done by the molester and the personal feelings about the molestation? Why or why not?

- Do you think it is important for children to face the past, or to forget about the past and get on with their own lives?

- Write one action you can take to teach your child that Jesus cares about all the things that happen to us.

Prayer for Comfort

O God, my child has a very difficult road to walk on. For too long this dear one has carried feelings of shame and humiliation alone. Help me to be a better listener to that pain. Help me to be the one to teach my child that you are the best listener of all. Amen.

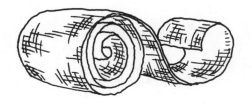

FOURTEENTH DAY

Death of Innocence

For the prayer corner:
A bandage made out of a torn white cloth.

*"Lazarus, come out!" The dead man came out, his hands and
feet bound with strips of cloth, and his face wrapped in a cloth.
Jesus said to them, "Unbind him, and let him go."*

(John 11:43-44)

Read John 11:1-25.

In the story of Lazarus it doesn't tell us exactly the nature of
Lazarus' sickness. We do know that Mary and Martha tried to
nurse him back to health. When they realized their brother needed more than the care of family members, they turned to the Master for help. They expected Jesus, who was known for his miraculous healings, to come at once to heal Lazarus. Jesus was just two
short miles from Bethany, but to the disciples' surprise, he did not
leave immediately. Instead he deliberately waited two days before
he left Jerusalem. When he finally arrived, Lazarus lay in the tomb.
As Christians, we feel abandoned if we do not sense the Lord's

presence at critical times in our lives. We feel deserted if he doesn't appear to be with us when we need him most, especially when we ask him to help a member of our family. Perhaps like Martha we keep our gaze on the distance, waiting for Jesus to return to our lives in a real and tangible way. We may fail to recognize that his Holy Spirit has never left us since his resurrection.

I found myself being drawn again and again to this passage in Scripture. I began to wonder how the resurrection of Lazarus related to my sexually abused child. Then as I meditated on the story, I became uncomfortably aware that a part of my child's emotional life had died as a result of the sexual abuse committed against her will. Her sexuality was imprinted and formed by acts of violence, and the memories of those encounters would stay with her a lifetime. In an effort to cope, my child locked herself into an emotional tomb by distancing herself from others. She became lifeless and lacked little if any joy in her life.

I mourned the emotional death of my child along with grieving for the death of her sexual innocence. I realized that, as my child grew to adulthood, she might not be able to relate to other human beings in a healthy emotional and sexual way. In addition, my child and I could not erase the fact that she was sexually abused as a child and that she might develop differently from other children. I felt scared and sad.

This realization brought tears to my eyes. As the tears fell, I brushed the water spots off the well-worn page of my Bible. My eyes caught the verse, "Jesus wept." Was it possible that Jesus could weep over the molestation of my child? Was his heart as broken as mine was for my child? Did he not love my child as much as he loved Lazarus? I believe the answer was yes to each of those questions.

Shortly afterward my child began seeing a sexual abuse therapist. I asked the Great Physician to return the feelings and life to my child. I repeated the prayer Jesus said when he prayed for Lazarus: " 'Father, I thank you for having heard me. I knew that you always hear me. . . .' Please call my child out of her tomb of darkness."

I also asked that her healing would be with one intent. In John 11:40 Jesus said, "Did I not tell you that if you believed, you would see the glory of God?" My one desire was that my child would be able to recognize that it was God who had called her to life again. I asked for my child to be a Lazarus, a walking miracle for others to see.

I prayed my Lazarus prayer over my child many years ago. I can't tell you how many relatives, teachers, and friends have said, "I can't believe she is the same child who was so broken when she first came to your family." I can, because I know it was the Lord who touched her in ways no human could. He called her to life, and she danced a song of praise as the bandages dropped to the ground.

* * *

Sometimes I Feel Sad

Dear Mom and Dad,

I have felt sad so many times, but I never felt as sad as the first day my uncle abused me. I felt as though someone had just killed someone I loved dearly. I guess in a way my uncle did kill someone. He killed me, because from that day I felt really bad. He also killed the relationship between him and me. From that day I didn't think of him as my uncle, but as someone who wanted to hurt me.

Love,
Marisol

Dear Marisol,

We are very sorry that your uncle has brought so much pain and sadness into your tender life. He must have hurt you very much for you to feel so sad. It also sounds like you are feeling sad because a part inside of you died.

Marisol, it's okay to feel sad when you think about your uncle and you. It's even okay to cry when you think about your past and the things that happened to you. Try to remember that feelings are not good or bad. Your feelings are just another wonderful part of you. I think God gave people feelings so they would have a way of expressing things that sometimes are too painful to talk about.

You are not the only one who feels sad about the decisions your uncle made. Both your father and I have cried because he hurt our daughter, whom we love very much. Maybe that is one of the reasons why we are so careful now about where you go and who you are with. We want to know you are safe. We don't want anyone else to harm you.

This is not a very happy time for any of us right now. And that's okay. But we do need to remember that life is not totally sad. There are some happy moments, too. Like right now when I am thinking of the joy you bring us just by being you! And we are glad that you have allowed us to give you the love you need right now. In fact, how about coming over for a hug when you finish this letter? I think we all need one!

Love,
Mom and Dad

Dear God,

Only you know how sad my heart is. It is a sadness I carry deep down inside of me. Sometimes I even keep how sad I feel a secret. I don't know why some of this sadness just doesn't go away. I just don't want to stay sad forever. Can you help me with my feelings, God?

Marisol

* * *

What Has Died in Your Child?

• What is the state of your child's emotional health (depressed, hostile, angry, fearful, isolated, unstable, insecure, worried, guilty, out of touch with feelings)?

• What does your child most need from you right now?

• Are you able to give that to your child?

- Jesus said, "I am the resurrection and the life" (John 11:25). Do you believe Jesus can call the life back into your child and family? If so, please write a prayer asking him to help your child.

Prayer for Life for your Child

- You may write your own prayer on this page.

FIFTEENTH DAY

Lost and Alone

For the prayer corner:
A picture of a lamb with cotton glued to it.

Which one of you, having a hundred sheep and losing one of them, does not leave the ninety-nine in the wilderness and go after the one that is lost until he finds it? When he has found it, he lays it on his shoulders and rejoices. (Luke 15:4-5)

There are seven words that can cut deeply into the heart of a sexually abused child: "I thought I was the only one." The strange and scary things that happen between a child and the molester are done in seclusion. The child often believes he or she is the only child in the world who has been touched in private places.

Children need to be taught that sexual abuse happens to many boys and girls and of all ages. Even after children have been told that the sexual abuse done to them was not their fault, it may not be enough to release the judgments they place on themselves. They need to hear these words of assurance again and again. And at different ages.

When I first discovered my child had been abused, I wanted to do everything I could to help make her feel better and fix her. I gave her special attention and bought her things, hoping they would make her happy. We were told the facts about her abuse, and there didn't seem to be anything else we needed to talk about. Once I recovered from the shock, I busied myself by taking care of my other children or sheep in my flock. I lost track of my one little lamb. I just assumed that with enough time and love, everything would somehow work out.

I must have been a little like the shepherd in the parable of the lost sheep. I thought all the sheep in my family were taken care of until I took the time to actually count them. While my child who had been abused had not run away, she had almost made herself invisible in the family. She had lost all trust in adults, and she tested me to my limits when I asked her to share any relationship with me which she viewed as threatening. I knew if I made an effort to search her out, it meant I would have to leave the ninety and nine and travel the distance and effort for the one. To be honest, I wasn't quite sure I wanted to do that. I was pretty worn out by our fighting.

I somehow thought, if I could just become a better parent, the aftereffects of the abuse on my child's behavior would go away. So I tried some new parenting techniques with my child. It was like putting a bandage on a person with a severed arm. I became increasingly frustrated.

I retreated to my prayer corner and angrily told God that he must have made a mistake in giving me this lamb. His answer came back loud and clear. In my spiritual ears I heard the words of a song, "If you love me, feed my lambs." I rapidly answered him, "Not this one, Lord. Not this lamb." The words "feed my lambs" stayed with me for weeks, and so did the anger.

Facing my anger was easier than facing my child. I started an exercise program and found someone to help me share my defeats and frustrations. I placed a picture of a lamb in my prayer corner and waited.

One day when I was feeling stronger and hopeful, I went looking for my lost sheep. I found her alone in her room. I asked, "Do you know that being a mother is like being a shepherd? It is my job to love you, take care of you, feed you, and protect you." I didn't expect her to say anything and she didn't. I continued, "Do you know that sometimes I think of you as a little woolly lamb?" She smiled, almost amused at the idea she could be a lamb.

"Sometimes you are a frisky lamb because you are always trying to hide from me. I think one of the reasons you are hiding is because you are feeling bad about some of the sad things that happened to you before you came to live with us." Her brown eyes blinked moisture at the direct hit.

"I think if I called you Lovey the Lamb you would know that even though some sad things happened to you that were not your fault, you are still a lovable person. In fact, I love you and want to spend time with you. I think if I gave you the nickname Lovey that would be one reminder I want to give you attention." Her head nodded up and down enthusiastically.

"Lovey," I said, "how about tonight after your bath, shall I read you a bedtime story about a little lost lamb?"

"I'd like that, Mommy. How soon can I go to bed?"

* * *

Has This Happened to Anyone Else?

Dear Mom and Dad,

When I think about what happened to me, I wonder if I'm the only person this happened to. If I'm the only person who has to live with this troubling feeling. I've heard of kids who have been hit a lot by their parents, but I haven't heard of anyone else who has the same story as I have. There probably are more people who have the same story as mine, but I just have not heard about them.

Love,
Marisol

Dear Marisol,

It is easy to believe that you are the only person in the world to whom this has happened. When you look around your family or classroom at school, you might think that no

70

one else has been mistreated. Well, you just might be wrong about that. Children grow up to be adults, and they still keep their memories—the good and the bad things that happen to them. They just don't go around wearing signs or clothing telling other people that some sad things happened to them when they were little.

I am sure there are other boys and girls at your school who have been touched against their wishes on the private parts of their body by someone they knew and trusted. The facts are that many children all over the world have had a scary and sad thing happen to them just like you.

Don't think for a moment that you are the only one in your school. Researchers tell us that if I were sitting at a table with four women, it is likely that two of them would have a secret or story to tell about their childhood. It is also possible that your story might be almost the same as their story. If your dad were sitting at a table with eight men, it is likely that one of the men had a sexual secret from his childhood.

Today more than at any time in history, people are writing and telling their own stories. It sounds to me like you need to know that you are not the only child in the world who has a story about good and bad touching. We'd like to take you to the library and show you the selection of books on childhood sexual abuse. There are some books that are written just for children so they can better understand what happened to them. Your father and I would like to read the library book with you just in case you have some more questions you may want to think about.

Marisol, you were right when you said you have a story. Perhaps on the way home from the library we can get some art supplies. When you are ready, you can start to make your very own story book about your uncle and you.

Love,
Mom and Dad

Dear God,

Now I know that there are hundreds, even thousands of kids with a story just like mine. I don't feel so all alone. I'm so glad I have my family and you on my side. I'm scared to draw the pictures of my uncle and me, but I think I am going to try. Will you be watching me?

Marisol

* * *

Littlest Lamb Prayer

You are the littlest lamb, and tonight you are going to talk to the Shepherd Jesus, the one who gives you life, who feeds you with his Word, who provides restful waters by the streams made with your tears. Littlest lamb, you like to speak to the Shepherd you know who made you.

Now it is time to tell the Shepherd about your day. Tell him one thing you did today. (Pause)

Now tell him something that made you happy. Did you walk on the grass and did it tickle your feet? (Pause)

Now you can tell the Shepherd about one of your feelings today. Was it mad, or sad, or glad, or scared? (Pause)

Maybe today you did something to hurt someone. Maybe it was not nice. Perhaps you want to tell God how sorry you are and ask for his forgiveness. Tell him now, and ask him to help you do better tomorrow. (Pause)

There are some people you may want to ask God to take care of, family or people you know very well. Or maybe you want God to help someone you don't know well. Just tell him what is inside your heart. (Pause)

And, Good Shepherd, we know you like to hear all the words we say because you are everywhere and you like to listen to the Littlest Lamb Prayer. Amen.

Physical Touch

For the prayer corner:
A bowl of water and a folded napkin or towel.

Then he poured water into a basin and began to wash the disciples' feet and to wipe them with the towel that was tied around him. (John 13:5)

Read John 13:1-17, 34-35.

On Holy Thursday, the night before Jesus was nailed to the cross, the disciples gathered in the upper room to celebrate the Passover feast. For three years these twelve men had followed Jesus, the young Jewish rabbi, from city to city observing miracle after miracle. Yet these disciples did not understand many things about their Teacher. They did not understand that this would be the last meal they would eat with the Master.

Peter was confused when he saw Jesus act like a common servant and wash the feet of the disciples. However, after Jesus explained the meaning behind the physical touch, Peter began to understand that Jesus desired his followers to reach out to humanity and touch the human condition by serving one another.

Two thousand years later Christians around the world continue to reenact the foot-washing service during Holy Week. Those who participate describe this ceremony as an action language of tenderness and compassion. Others say they are rededicated to the ministry of serving others, especially those in their family.

James experienced foot washing at his church for the first time last Easter. The service began with the pastor asking the participants to pray for one hurting person in their life. James immediately thought of his son David, who was abducted by a stranger one morning as he walked to school. He was raped almost every night by his assailant until he escaped a year ago. Police picked him up in another city when he tried to sell himself to an undercover cop, and then the boy was reunited with his family. David, who just turned twelve, had now been home for six months.

James began the foot-washing service on his knees. His partner, a man, sat in a chair. James lifted his partner's bare feet over the water basin, then he gently cupped the water and let it run down the sides of the foot into the basin. He thought about David, wondering about all the places his son's feet took him in the four years he lived with the kidnapper. Slowly he took his hand and gently guided the foot of his partner into the basin, letting it rest awhile in the lukewarm water. He massaged the toes carefully with his hands, then reached for a cotton towel. Ever so gently, he guided the feet out of the water and rested them in the warmth and security of the towel. At that moment James longed to be a parent to David, one who could offer him rest and security from the past. He prayed that God would give him a servant's heart for his son.

As James dried his partner's feet, he found himself a little embarrassed and scared by the close physical contact he experienced in the foot-washing service. He finished quickly, almost abruptly. Later, when he was alone with his thoughts, he related to his son's feelings for the first time. Close physical contact initiated out of love and legitimate caring is scary for most people. It is possible that David always would be reserved and never allow anyone to express affection to him, especially his father.

James was not a parent to give up the direction the Lord was taking him. Instead, he courageously accepted the fact that David was confused by physical touching and intimacy. Whether David acted like it or not, he did need a father. In James's prayer corner, he placed a bowl of water and a small hand towel. He could not take David by the hand and wash his feet or his hands anymore as he did when he was little. Yet he certainly could hold strong in his mind and heart the desire to serve and take care of him to the best of his ability. Just being together was enough for now.

But What About Me?

By Kathy Woods[2]

Now I lay me down to sleep
The bible tells us
what we sow
is what we reap. . . .
Obey your parents
That's right in the Lord
Daddy says. . . .
"the Bible is sharper
than a two edged sword"
And I obey him
as he holds the Bible over my head
as he puts his hot sweaty body
close to mine in my little bed.
He tells me that it's not wrong
but that I can't tell,
No One would believe me
Am I going to Hell???
I try to make him stop
but he's bigger than me
the Whole Church Loves Him
but what about Me???

* * *

What Makes the Person so Different?

Dear Mom and Dad,
   I wonder why my uncle was so different from the rest of my relatives? I wish he could have showed me his love by giving me a hug, or just a kiss on the cheek. I keep asking myself why he didn't go to another grown-up. Whatever the reason, I wish somebody would explain it to me.
      Love,
      Marisol

Dear Marisol,
   You are asking a question that is difficult to answer. The hard part for me is talking about people who are so different from you and I. There are millions of people in the world. People are not all the same. Their faces are different. The skin colors are different. Even the languages they speak are different. We are different from each other, and your uncle is different too, but in another way.
   Your uncle has a different way of looking at children than most of the other people in the world look at children. Maybe he was feeling bad and thought that doing those things with you would make him feel better, even if the things he did hurt you. I don't think he thought too much about your feelings or about what he was doing. Your uncle was probably thinking about his own wants. I think he made some selfish decisions that have hurt you very much. I'm so sorry that your uncle didn't get some help from adults for his problems.
   Some doctors study the human mind and the way people think. They tell us there are a small number of people in the world who want to touch children on the private parts of their bodies and do sexual things with them. They also tell us these people can be men or women. Sometimes they are older boys or older girls. Most of the people in the world

want to love and protect children. They are not interested in using children for their own emotional and sexual satisfaction.

People who touch children on the private parts of their bodies are called child molesters. Doctors don't have all the answers to the questions we have about child molesters, but they are working hard and learning more and more every year. They are learning how and why people want to use children for their own pleasure. They are finding new ways to help child molesters change their behavior so the world is a safer place for children.

Marisol, you may never know exactly why your uncle was different from the rest of your relatives or the reasons why he chose you. There is one thing you can know: The things that happened between you and your uncle happened because your uncle had some problems. He knew what he was doing was wrong, and it wasn't your fault that he made you do things that made you feel uncomfortable. I hope one day your uncle will accept the fact that he is different from other people and get some help from a doctor.

Your father and I also think you are very brave for coming to us to get some answers to your questions. We know it isn't always easy to talk about your thoughts and feelings, but we appreciate the fact you are trying.

Love,
Mom and Dad

Dear God,

I don't exactly understand why my uncle has problems and is different from most people. Sometimes I get a headache when I think about what happened between my uncle and me. Sometimes I just want to forget it ever happened. The fact is, I'm doing my best to talk to you about it. Thanks for listening, God. I really need you now.

Marisol

* * *

I Don't Want to Talk About It

- Even after a child begins therapy for the sexual abuse, it is surprising how many parents have little or no information about the actual abuse committed. It is not uncommon for parents to say they don't know the specific acts the molester perpetrated against their child, how many times, or for how many years.

- Has your child told you all or most of the sexual abuse he or she experienced? Why or why not?

- Has it been difficult for you to talk about details of the sexual abuse with your child or his/her therapist?

- You may find these suggestions helpful:

[ ] Ask the child to make a silent book about the abuse and write an explanation under the picture. Give the book to a parent to read. (Good for any age of child.)

[ ] Ask the child to draw pictures of any threats the molester may have made and explain the picture to the parent. Assure your child he/she is safe and protected today.

[ ] Tell your child you want to reopen the discussion about the sexual abuse done to him/her when he/she was younger. You want it to be an open subject, and you want to sit down together weekly, biweekly, or monthly and get the facts you never received at the beginning.

[ ] Schedule some joint sessions with the child and therapist so that the therapist can support the child's telling the details.

Prayer for Open Communication

- You may write a prayer asking God to help you open the lines of communication between youself and your child.

Healing
the Hurting
Child

What is impossible for mortals is possible for God.
—Luke 18:27

SEVENTEENTH DAY

The Parent's Role

For the prayer corner: Open your Bible to Luke 8:40.

Just then there came a man named Jairus, a leader of the synagogue. He fell at Jesus' feet and begged him to come to his house, for he had an only daughter, about twelve years old, who was dying. (Luke 8:41-42)

Read Luke 8:40-42, 49-56.

Jairus, a religious man, knew who to turn to and how to find assistance for his child. Two thousand years later, people of faith continue to seek Jesus when their children have a crisis. Often, like the dying daughter, they are exhausted and unable to come for assistance themselves. Children rely on their parents to do something for them to alleviate the physical or emotional pain in which they find themselves.

Relief must have flooded through Jairus' body when Jesus left immediately to help his daughter, but Jesus was interrupted in his healing mission. First, the crowd pressed against him so hard he was detained. Second, the woman with the issue of blood received a healing before Jairus' daughter, and she delays Jesus by telling him about twelve years of illness. Scripture is telling us that Jesus, capable of healing and desiring to heal, often does not answer our specific requests when a crisis strikes our families, even in life-and-death situations.

Jairus probably wondered if Jesus was going to make it in time before his daughter died. He didn't have to wonder long because a messenger soon came from his house, saying, "Your daughter is dead. Don't bother the teacher any more."

Jairus didn't get angry with Jesus and blame him for the delays. He didn't respond negatively or positively to the news from his servant that his daughter had died. Instead, he accepted the words the Rabbi gave him: "Don't be afraid; just believe, and she will be healed" (Luke 8:50, NIV). Together they continued to the home of Jairus. From this Scripture, Jesus is teaching us that our fears are calmed and our faith strengthened when we choose to walk side by side with him in any situation.

Sometimes because of the years of abuse my child suffered and the ongoing problems this abuse brings, most people doubt God's ability to heal my child. There are well-meaning people, some of them religious, who mourn the death of my child's innocence but lack the faith to encourage me that Jesus can help my child's healing process. To my friends, things like recovery and wholeness seem out of the realm of possibilities for a sexually abused child. They are probably no different from those friends at the house of Jairus; their mourning turned to laughter at the ridiculous idea of changing the lot of a dead child. Instead of being angry and resentful, I pray the Lord to send me a Jairus to walk with me past the ignorance of others.

Jesus demonstrated his great mercy and compassion toward children by restoring the daughter of Jairus to life. In addition, he instructed the parents to give her something to eat. Jesus could have prescribed a special herb. He could have asked for food and fed her. Instead, he gave her parents the responsibility of providing nourishing food for her. The child's recovery was based on Jesus and the parents *working together* to restore and strengthen the little girl.

In a real way Jairus, the religious leader, fed his daughter spiritual food when he lived his faith at home. She tasted firsthand a spiritual nugget many adults never experience. With God's help and assistance from others, Lord willing, you can receive a healing. This is the kind of faith-food of which miracles are made.

Oh, how I long to keep a strong faith over the years like Jairus, who left his tasks and pleaded with the Lord to restore his child to health and recovery. I want a faith that will follow my child in prayer and petitions into adulthood. But for now, it is enough for me to believe that the words my Lord spoke to Jairus 2,000 years ago still ring true, "Have faith, and your child shall be restored."

Prayer of Healing

O God, I thank you that you love (child's name) and gave this dear one to us, and that we are the family you have chosen to love and nurture this child in Christ. I ask that you strengthen us, the parents, with a special understanding, patience, acceptance, and love so that we may be one of the instruments you use to bring healing and peace to our child.

O God, the giver of life and healing, I bring (child's name) who has been hurt physically, emotionally, and spiritually by another person. I ask for your healing upon my child. I know my child can never forget the past, but I am asking you, Jesus, to comfort (child's name) and soften the painful memories. Please touch the wounded part with your tender hands of mercy. Amen.

And His Ears Were Opened

For the prayer corner:
The word *Ephphatha* written on a piece of paper.

He took him aside in private, away from the crowd, and put his fingers into his ears, and he spat and touched his tongue. Then looking up to heaven, he sighed and said to him, "Ephphatha," that is, "Be opened." (Mark 7:33-34)

Read Mark 7:32-37.

Rosemary's daughter Jill moved out-of-state to go to college and Rosemary felt hurt that she did not keep in contact with the family. Jill didn't even send a Mother's Day card. Rosemary knew they had not always been the best of friends, but she wondered why her daughter chose to hurt her so.

Because the previous year had also been filled with unexplainable tension, Rosemary decided the time had come to clear the air. She wrote Jill and asked her to reveal the problem with their relationship.

Jill let her mother have it. She dumped her secret right in the middle of her mother's lap—the fact that her stepfather had sexually abused her for years. The information did not come as a complete surprise to Rosemary. Before she married Joe she knew he looked at *those kinds of books*. He kept them in the basement and told her, "Don't worry about them. They are nothing but a bunch of books I like to look at once in a while."

Rosemary's stomach felt uneasy, and she followed her instinct to go down to the basement. She pulled the workbench drawer open where Joe kept *"the stuff."* Right on top of the pile was a well-worn kiddie porno magazine. Suddenly a memory from the past flooded her mind. She was alone in the bedroom and heard Joe walking up the basement stairs. Instead of coming to their room, he went into Jill's room to say good-night. He stayed in her room a long time. Way too long!

Rosemary was angry now. She slammed the drawer and headed upstairs to confront her husband. She threw the letter at him and asked for an explanation.

Joe denied that anything ever happened between them. He forbade her daughter to ever set foot in their house again if she came back carrying such outrageous tales. He didn't want to hear about *IT*, and didn't have anything to say about *IT*. As far as he was concerned, *IT* was a closed discussion in *his* house. Period.

A family wound and secret had been reopened, and it was just too painful for both of them to deal with. Rosemary closed her eyes and ears to the truth. After all, her complete marriage and future was at stake. She was simply too weak and scared to make a life for herself at retirement age. She and Joe had not had sexual relations for years. Jill was the last child to leave home, so who else could her husband hurt now? She stayed.

Rosemary wrote her daughter and told her, "That was a long time ago. Maybe it would be best for everyone to just forgive and forget."

Thus we have a family of deaf mutes who all need a miraculous healing. Jill's father continues to deny that the abuse ever took place and is unwilling to discuss the matter at all. Many child molesters, when confronted by adults who were sexually abused as children, do not acknowledge the offense or ask for forgiveness. Often the relationship remains broken.

Rosemary enables her husband to keep his secret and puts other children at risk unless she opens her eyes to the reality of sex offenders. Statistics on incest reveal the *"other parent"* is often aware of the abuse but does not confront it. Healing cannot take place in this family until Rosemary recognizes that she didn't protect her child.

Jill, rightfully so, carries anger against both of her parents. She needs to hear her mother ask for forgiveness for not coming to her aid and protecting her from her stepfather's abuse. Both of her parents are part of the vital components which Jill needs in order to recover. Until they all work together, their child Jill remains wounded and unable to heal fully.

Recently Rosemary received a letter from her daughter:

Dear Mother,

I joined a group for Survivors of Sexual Abuse. I borrowed a book from the therapist who leads our sessions. I discovered something very interesting. Many incest survivors repeat my family's story. The mother is not able to protect or comfort her child, the father denies his responsibility for the sexual abuse, and the marriage stays together. I am very angry about what both of my parents did to me. But I also feel sorry for you, Mom. I just wish you would hear the truth and admit this awful thing has happened to me.

Your daughter,
Jill

Rosemary opened her Bible to the story of the deaf man. As she placed Jill's letter on the page, she decided she would try to be a better parent today than she was yesterday. She asked God to touch her, starting with her ears.

Three Blind Mice

• Have you confronted the person who molested your child? Did that offender deny the incident or acknowledge it?

• How has the denial or acknowledgment made your child feel?

• Are other children or grandchildren at risk because your family cannot acknowledge a member is a child molester? Explain.

• Check one action you can take to face the situation.

[ ] Acknowledge your family has a sexual abuse secret.
[ ] Tell my child I believe that he/she was sexually abused.
[ ] Educate my children and grandchildren on sexual abuse prevention.
[ ] Confront the sex offender with the truth about his/her behavior.
[ ] Suggest counseling and offer support to the sex offender.

Prayer of Acknowledgment

O God, giver of all things, please give me courage to face the truth. And with this truth may I in one small action bring some peace to this situation. Amen.

NINETEENTH DAY

Letting Go

For the prayer corner: A small woven basket.

The woman conceived and bore a son; and when she saw that he was a fine baby, she hid him three months. When she could hide him no longer she got a papyrus basket for him, and plastered it with bitumen and pitch; she put the child in it and placed it among the reeds on the bank of the river. (Exodus 2:2-3)

Read Exodus 2:1-10.

Hebrew parents had no choice but to live in a society where a Pharaoh's decree decided, by the sex of a child, who should live and who should die at birth. An injustice against innocent children claimed the life of many newborn boys as they were thrown into the Nile River to die. Fear was the driving force behind Rameses' decision. He reasoned that if the Egyptians killed only boy babies, there would not be anyone for the girls to marry. There would be no new Hebrew families, and no threat of over-population and a possible revolution against the ruling party.

Courageously, one Hebrew slave woman dared to stand against

the order of the Pharaoh and protect the life of her newborn son. It doesn't state in Scripture that Jochebed (Exodus 6:20) had a revelation from the Almighty or an ounce of faith in God. In fact, she actually put her son in the very river that would have been his burial place had he been discovered by an Egyptian soldier. It was our merciful God who took care of her baby and spared his life. Sometimes a parent has no choice but to place a child adrift in very dangerous waters, hoping, when hope has not revealed itself, that somehow it will all work out.

Betty never imagined she would say the "Baby Moses" prayer over her son. Just a few years before, she and her husband, Mark, were so happy as they left the hospital with their new baby, Robin. Last fall Mark was promoted to shop foreman at his parents' flag factory in Canada. Often his grandparents took Robin to New York on business trips. They loved to spoil him with presents. Betty had everything she wanted. She thought.

One morning Betty was giving her four-year-old son a bath when he reached for the washcloth and began to rub himself roughly. Betty reached to take the washcloth away from him, but he protested, saying, "Please Mommy, let's play Daddy's game." He continued to rub his small erect penis with his hand.

A terrible feeling came over Betty as questions raced through her mind. Did my child say "Daddy's game"? Could my husband be a . . . a . . . ? She couldn't bring herself to say the words *child molester*. Instead, she cupped her hand over her mouth, fearing the vomit would come up as she leaned closer to the toilet. When she turned around to look at Robin pushing his tugboat in the bubbles, he looked so tiny and helpless to her.

Maybe Robin is just a little mixed-up today, she thought. So she questioned him further, "Honey, does Daddy like to give you baths?"

"Oh yes, Mommy! He says his daddy used to give him baths when he was a little boy. That's how he learned the washcloth game."

A bolt of anger shot through Betty's body as she grabbed Robin by the arm and pulled him from the tub. "Here, dry yourself off! I am going to call your father this very minute."

Mark said, "Robin was wrong, so wrong he'd be dead wrong if

he didn't change his story." He told Betty to tell Robin to get the belt out because when he got home he intended to give him a spanking he wouldn't forget. And Betty better stay out of it!

Betty hung up the phone and gave Robin the third degree. There was no doubt in her mind that someone had taught her son things he could not have known. As far as she was concerned, that someone was her husband.

The hands on the clock were moving closer to 3:00 p.m. She knew it was payday and Mark always stopped off at the bar to cash his check. That meant that if she was going to do anything to protect herself and Robin, she had only a couple of hours left. Time was ticking down. Was it going to be Mark and violence, or Robin and safety?

Betty was afraid to telephone her sister in another state because Mark would be angry about the phone bill. Instead, she went to the neighbor in the apartment below theirs. She was a kindly woman. Betty didn't tell her everything—just enough for them to figure out what to do. Together they collected Robin's clothes, his favorite blanket, and his teddy bear. Betty didn't have much to pack. Everything fit into one suitcase. The neighbor drove them to a women's shelter.

The staff at the Christian safe house did an intake interview. This time Betty was encouraged not to leave any information out. They advised her of the law—a report would have to be filed with child protective services charging her husband with child molestation. Should she and Robin decide to stay, free counseling would be provided for both of them.

Betty chose protection and safety for Robin. They continued to live at the safe house. Mark denied that he did anything to his child, and there was no evidence a molestation had occurred. Robin was too young to testify in court. Later, Betty filed for divorce and won custody of Robin. The divorce decree stated that the father had limited visitation rights.

Betty has never doubted for a minute that her husband was justly accused of sexual abuse. She is certain that if she allows Robin to visit his father, she will be putting him at risk. If Betty denies him visitation, she could be charged with contempt of court and thrown into jail.

She is quite similar to Moses' mother, who had power and authority dictating the future of her child. Betty is torn between going underground and protecting her child, or following the law and allowing Robin visitation with his father. It is a decision no parent should have to face.

In her suitcase Betty keeps a small woven basket. It was a gift from one of the staff members at the shelter. The card reads:

The Baby Moses Prayer

Dear God, you care about every mother's concerns. You look down upon the smallest of children. If this mother chooses to hide her child, please provide them with your protection. If this child must have contact with someone who could harm the child, please, God, send a person who can bring peace and comfort to the child in the midst of confused feelings. Amen.

A Time of Silence

For all mothers and fathers
who have to
let their children go
into dangerous water.

TWENTIETH DAY

Victory Day

For the prayer corner:
A Y-shaped twig, a rubber band, and five stones.

Then he took his staff in his hand, and chose five smooth stones from the wadi, and put them in his shepherd's bag, in the pouch; his sling was in his hand, and he drew near to the Philistine.

(1 Samuel 17:40)

Read 1 Samuel 17:1-51.

Jerry flipped the calender page over and read the date: June 1—ten years from the date he had married Marilyn. So much had changed since then and for the worse. Marilyn became disenchanted and disappointed with Christianity. For a while she dabbled in the Eastern religions, and then she turned to the giant of the dark side of religion. She became a Satanist.

Jerry asked her to choose: her religion, or him and their child Richard. Marilyn chose to stay in service to Satan. Jerry filed for divorce and won custody of Richard. After he got custody of their son, Jerry found out that Marilyn was not just taking Richard to baby-sitting when she went to services. No, Richard's little body was being used as part of the sexual rituals in the high mass. Jerry filed criminal charges against his wife, and the court ordered sexual abuse counseling immediately for their son.

The giant of Richard's sexual abuse and emotional problems stood between his past and his future, just as Goliath stood between the people of Israel and the Philistines. The young boy lived in fear day and night of Satan and his dark and evil powers.

His father felt paralyzed as he sat on the sidelines like the Israelites who were unwilling to face the giant. He was overwhelmed by the additional responsibility of parenting a sexually abused child. For him, war is not an option, not even against a giant. A caring friend encouraged Jerry to go to counseling. Here he picked up two of the five stones he needed to face the giant problems that stood before him and his son. The two stones were *confrontation* and *communication*.

The only person Jerry trusted with his son was his mother. Every week on his way to counseling, he took Richard to her house. Grandma bought a Christian coloring book, and together she and Richard colored the pictures. Sometimes she read him Bible stories. Before long, seven-year-old Richard was asking her questions about *"HIM, the awful one."*

About two years later a discouraged Jerry came over to his mother's house. He was doing all he could to undo the damage in his son's life and his own. Jerry had finished his counseling, but Richard would float in and out of counseling for years. Then Jerry's mother asked him if he would consider returning to the church he attended as a child. She would go with him and Richard that Sunday. "Evil can never be fought with evil. No, it must be conquered with a power greater than evil," she told him.

Jerry nervously dressed for church. It had been years since he practiced his religion. Little Richard was scared to get out of the car, but after Jerry convinced him that he would hold his hand and wouldn't let anything bad happen to him, the boy was able to cautiously enter the church.

Jerry felt the sermon "David and Goliath" was meant just for him. He learned that the smallest amount of faith, even the most childlike, is enough for any problem he or his loved ones would

93

face. David, because he knew the God of Israel, believed God's protection shielded him from his fears. He had mastered a spiritual truth: When the Lord is called upon, he helps the helpless conquer the giant problems in their lives.

On the way home Grandma assured young Richard that the Christian church was not a dark place of violence. No, it was a place to find rest and peace for the sad things that happen that are not our fault.

Later, Jerry called the pastor and told him the sermon had encouraged him with his personal problems. The pastor told him that beginning next month he would teach a class on "Using Spiritual Weapons When Facing Life's Problems." He invited Jerry to join the class. In the meantime, he welcomed Jerry and his son to return next Sunday to worship with them. Jerry felt hopeful about the future.

How to Confront a Giant

• Sometimes giant problems are created because a person has not been able to face events in the past and they are dictating present behavior. Any giant can be conquered with God's power; here is a way to go forward.

• *Name the giant.* Identify the biggest problem in your child's life.

• *Decide to face the giant with courage.* "God, grant me the serenity to accept the things I cannot change, the courage to change the things I can, and the wisdom to know the difference."

• *Use the Lord's protection as your shield.* "The Lord is my help and my protection; in him do I trust."

• *You cannot move with the great weight of military clothing.* Daily I decide to wear the spiritual clothing of a peacemaker.

• *Use the weapons you are familiar with.* "Faith, hope, and love . . . and the greatest of these is love."

• *Do not get too close to the giant.* I take one step backward and count to ten before I advance again.

- *Believe kingdom living is not won with sword and spear.* " 'Not by might, nor by power, but by my spirit,' says the Lord."

- *Speak the name of the Lord to deliver the giant into his hands.* "Oh God, you are my help in time of trouble; in you do I trust."

Prayer for Courage

O God, help me and my child. The problems are gigantic and we are so helpless. Only with your assistance can we face the truths. Amen.

TWENTY-FIRST DAY

The Forgiveness Tree

For the prayer corner: A shoot of evergreen, set up as a tree.

As God's chosen ones, holy and beloved, clothe yourselves with compassion, kindness, humility, meekness, and patience. Bear with one another and, if anyone has a complaint against another, forgive each other; just as the Lord has forgiven you.

(Colossians 3:12-13)

Read Luke 19:1-10.

Zacchaeus, the hated chief tax collector of Jericho, was excluded from religious services because he was working for the ruling foreigners, the Romans. He was the last person a rabbi would choose to talk with and share a meal with. From a human perspective, Zacchaeus was an untouchable, yet Jesus reached out to touch him. Jesus called him down from the sycamore tree and went with him to visit in his home. Zacchaeus found what all of us look for when we feel unlovable and rejected: someone, especially a significant other, whose words conveyed acceptance and love.

Jesus sought out and invited Zacchaeus to be in relationship with him, even though Zacchaeus had the reputation of being a sinner. Someone wisely said, "God hates the sin, but never the sinner."

I remember feeling like I was a horrible sinner and Jesus couldn't possibly want anything to do with me. I hated the man who hurt my child. As I projected my feelings of hatred onto my child, I hated the mother I was turning into. Hate was consuming my world. I took my anger out on the target of least resistance—my silent hurting child. I spoke cruel words which cut into her spirit like a hacking kitchen knife, cutting sharp and to the bone. My tongue had become, as the Bible says, like a raging fire that can't be stopped until tremendous damage has been done.

Other times my body language sent a loud and clear message: rejection. Once, after a confrontation I started, I caught sight of my face in a mirror. I was horrified at the *other woman's reflection*. I was no longer a woman of peace, but a woman of war. My child and I were both casualties. Our relationship had fallen apart, and the only glue that could mend it was Spiritual Superglue.

That is when I decided I would have to find a way to *"give—for"* my own self-preservation and sanity. I would have to find a way to *"give—for"* my child's emotional hurt and pain I had inflicted on her. I would have to admit my weaknesses and ask *forgiveness* for my aggressive and unacceptable behavior toward my daughter. I would have to ask God's *forgiveness* for my sinful behavior.

I invited my daughter to a forgiveness party. We planned our menu. Two Coca-Colas and M & M's. Together we walked to the lake near our home and picked out an amber green pine tree to spread our blanket under.

"Angelica," I said, "I have something I want to tell you. Sometimes I misuse my anger and take it out on you. I act like a mean, roaring lion. I really don't want to be that kind of Mommy to you. I told you something that was a lie. I said, 'I wish I had never adopted you.' I know I said it, but I didn't mean it."

Angelica pulled the string on her pant leg. Her head bent down and tears dropped on the plaid wool blanket.

Nervously I continued, "I'm sure that really hurt your feelings, especially when it wasn't true. Adoption isn't easy and being a

97

good parent is hard work. What I wanted to say was, 'I wish you were my little girl from the very beginning! I wish your uncle hadn't tricked you and hurt you in El Salvador.' Would you forgive me for lying? I'm sorry I hurt you with my words."

She said, "Of course, Mommy. I love you. And I think you can do better, too. Mommy, I want to ask your forgiveness for something, too."

I'm Sorry

• The act of forgiveness is like having spiritual surgery performed on us. When we can go to another person, especially a child, and ask for forgiveness, we are letting God allow us to experience a new relationship.

• Have you harmed your child in any way (physically, emotionally, or mentally)? If so, describe your actions.

• Are you willing to make changes in your life to reduce the stress and tensions that helped contribute to your lack of control (stress reduction class, parenting class, exercise, change of diet, etc.)?

Asking for Forgiveness

• Some parents may want to make this request right away. Others may want to wait for a more suitable time or place. Follow the leading of the Holy Spirit:

(Child's name), I was feeling (frightened, overwhelmed, shocked, paralyzed by grief or shock, etc.) when you told me about the sexual things between you and (the sex offender's name). I ask your forgiveness for any of my actions that caused you pain (not believing you, not protecting you, not defending you, or not coming to your aid). I also ask your forgiveness for all those words that were said out of (fear, ignorance, anger, guilt, etc.) and out of my confusion. (Child's name), I didn't intend to cause you pain and I'm very sorry if I burdened you unfairly. I love you. I want you to depend on that.

TWENTY-SECOND DAY

A Liturgy for a Lost Childhood

By Marty Green[3]

For the prayer corner: A tiny bouquet of flowers.

Introduction

When, after more than 30 years of amnesia and three years of therapy, I finally was able to remember the abuse of my childhood, part of me longed for some ritual to bring closure to this part of my life, to celebrate the present, and to prepare the way to get on with the future.

I discovered a longing for those social customs someone receives who has had a child die, because a part of me, my child, was killed. In our area, it is the custom to have announcements printed up on little cards telling of a person's death and funeral services. These cards are placed in local stores and mark the public acknowledgment that a loss has occurred. I wanted that public acknowledgment. I wanted the neighbors to bring home-baked goods to the house, to have a wake and funeral. I wanted my family to grieve with me. That isn't going to happen.

Instead, a prayer emerged from inside of me. It is for incest survivors, not incest victims. We *were* victimized. But now we *have* survived and can begin to heal. This prayer has helped my healing process. I offer it here, for any others who need a ritual of closure to a similar past.

The Memory

he is here. he is with me. i lie on his
arm. i like that. then he lies on my arm. i
don't like that so much. it hurts. it is too
heavy. but he is with me. he pays attention.

now we play that game again. he is
here. there. close. closer. it feels good.
now it doesn't feel good.
now I don't feel at all.

then he goes away. i don't know what
i did. mama is mad and daddy is gone.
i must have been so bad he left.
i just can't remember what i did.
and mama hates me for being with
daddy.

i don't know the words for this.
but inside, my body remembers,
down there, where memories still hurt.

The Prayer

God, all of these years I have felt evil, only I never knew quite why. I've tried to convince myself and others of how bad I am. I always thought it was confession I needed, but it never took away the guilt. Now that I've remembered the incest, I know it is healing I need from you, not forgiveness from others. I thought I needed to say. "Bless me, Father, for I have sinned." Now I know I need to say, "Bless me, for my father sinned."

Marty, you are not alone. Turn to me within yourself, search for me in community. Healing is possible. Keep trying, Marty, I am near to broken hearts and I am close to you.

God, my heart is surely broken. It is so hard to trust others, even you. Help me be open. Help me understand about anger. I'm so angry at *him* for what he did to me. I'm so angry at *them*, that I never even knew I deserved their love.

I was taught that anger is a sin. Admitting this rage makes me feel evil all over again. I need to learn it is a part of being human, not a sign of my wickedness.

Marty, listen to me. You have a right to your anger. Your loss is tremendous, but I do understand. I will help you heal.

But God! I missed out on so much. I want to have had a happy childhood. I want a mother and father who love me. Oh God, I want what I can never have.

What they did to you is wrong. But now you are making your own choices for the future. You are building a new life in the light of my love. I am very proud of you. Do not despair. I have been with you and I promise to remain with you.

I want to believe. Each day I choose for the future, but it was so hard to remember the pain and anger that sometimes I can't let it go for fear of forgetting again. How do I live without pain, without anger, without a family? I just can't do it by myself.

I promise you this: I am your light and your salvation. You need not fear. I will never leave you. I will never desert you. Even though your father and mother deserted you, I will always care for you. You can believe me; you will see goodness in life. Put your hope in me. Be strong.

I do try, God, but I feel such overwhelming failure. Again and again. I slip back and no longer want to live. Please, God, are you sure it's worth the struggle? Do you even remember that I'm here?

Hush, Marty. Does a woman forget her baby, or fail to cherish the daughter of her womb? Yet even if these forget, I will never forget you. It will be all right. I'm here.

Okay, I will begin again. While the incest was forgotten, I could not heal. Now I know. Thank you, God, that now I know. Thanks for the memories . You always did know and you never left me. I don't understand that very well, but thank you. I will try to believe in you and—so much harder—believe in myself. Together we will heal, one day at a time. Thanks, God, for sticking around.

Epilogue

I still hurt
sometimes, God.
I know, Marty.
I cannot, in
this scheme of things,
stop the hurting.
But, my child,
I can
I will
I do
hold you
close
to me
and
My touch
you can trust
for ever
and ever.
Amen.

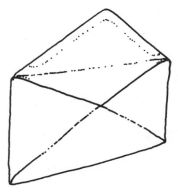

TWENTY-THIRD DAY

A Gift of Love

For the prayer corner: An empty envelope.

Therefore be imitators of God, as beloved children, and live in love, as Christ loved us and gave himself up for us, a fragrant offering and sacrifice to God. (Ephesians 5:1-2)

One of the most priceless gifts you can give is your word of encouragement, support, and love to a hurting child. Sometimes as parents, especially after a crisis, we may overlook a simple gift of healing that many survivors of sexual abuse need in order to recover. Whether they are seven or seventy years old, a letter will be welcomed and cherished for years.

Think of your child as an envelope. If the envelope is empty and isn't addressed to anyone, then it is not important to anyone. Children who were sexually abused often feel empty, misplaced, and rejected.

If something is put inside the envelope, it becomes valuable. One of the most valuable letters you can write is a love letter. Only you can write the letter your child needs to read. Below are some suggestions that will help heal your child's past. Take a moment and ask the Holy Spirit to help you write just the words your child longs to hear from you.

Suggestions

You may find help in these sample sentences:

- I was so caught up in my own confusion and anger that I didn't realize how badly you needed me for support. I'm sorry, (child's name), I didn't give it to you then, but I'm able to give my support to you now.

- I know it took a lot of courage for you to tell what happened to you. (Child molester's name) knew what he (or she) was doing was wrong, and it wasn't your fault he (or she) made you do things that caused you to feel uncomfortable.

- I'm sorry I didn't believe you when you told me the truth about being molested. I want you to know how sorry I am that you were molested.

- When you tried to tell me that you were having a problem with (child molester's name), I did a very selfish thing. I denied your pain and pretended our family didn't have a problem. I can't take back the years of pain I caused you. But I would like to help and support you in any way I can today.

- The things that happened to you with (child molester's name) were not your fault. You were an innocent victim of sexual abuse.

- When I found out that you were molested, I felt so guilty that I withdrew my emotional support from you. In addition, I allowed you to carry the burden of sexual abuse alone. At a time when you needed a parent most, I could not be there for you. I'd like you to give me a second chance.

A Letter of Thanks

Dear Mom and Dad,

I'm so glad I have parents who are able to listen to me and are willing to help me. I know that many children don't have a chance to talk or get help, so having you makes me feel lucky, like I found the rarest coin and it is worth a lot of money. I can't put my thanks to you in words because it's too great to be put in words. When I grow up, I may be good at helping other sexually abused kids. I'm glad my parents care about me so much to care and help me, and to let me have the facts about it. I feel a lot better, knowing my secrets are out. I wish other kids were as lucky as I am. Thanks a million.

Angelica

A Letter to My Adult Child

My Child,

I am writing you this letter because the day has come for you to find your own place and purpose in God's wonderful world. As you prepare to leave your family and go out and make a life of your own, I want to write my thoughts to you about the sexual abuse you experienced as a child. I'll never understand the reasons why sex offenders do sexual things to innocent children when they know they are wrong and against the law. I'm thankful that you are not carrying the blame. You have learned and believed that the things which happened with you and (sex offender's name) were not your fault.

I've considered it my greatest privilege and highest calling as a parent to stand with you in your pain. To wipe your tears and to show you hope. Now as you leave the security and safety of your family, I urge you to continue to tell your story to others.

If you choose marriage, your husband will want to be your comfort and strength as we were. The only way he can do that will be if you tell him your story before you are married. Your father and I would want to help you tell your story to him because we know how hard that will be.

I am glad you have saved all of your journals over the years. These may be used as tools should you *later* decide to return to group or private therapy. Whether or not you choose marriage, it is important that you place yourself with other survivors of sexual abuse. Depending upon your needs, you may choose individuals or an organization to help you. Your past will always stay alive in you unless you find ways and people to put it in its proper perspective and place in your life.

Remember, God sent his greatest comforter to each and every one of us. The Holy Spirit will be with you in whatever need you have at any time. No matter what city you live in or travel to, there will be a telephone prayer partner for you. The Christian radio or television stations can give you the phone number. When you reach out to Christian people to support you in your pain, you will sense God's wonderful presence around you.

My child, the world is full of ignorant educated people who continue to blame children for the sexual abuse done to them against their will. That is a sad fact we have to live with. All you have to do is open the morning newspaper and read about the injustices done to children by child molesters. Courageously step forward, if not with your voice, then with your pen. You can write letters to the editor, the victim's parents, the sex offender, lawyers, and judges. A person can never say too many times, "A child is never responsible for the sexual assault." The sin of sexual violence and the blame always goes where it belongs, and that is on the sex offender.

I'd like to leave you with one closing thought which I

kept ever-present in my mind as I watched you change and heal: "My daughter is as healed as she can be at this time in her life." I repeated this at different stages of your healing. I don't know anyone, myself included, who has reached a point in life where total healing of life's wounds has miraculously happened. No, the sexual abuse that was done to you will always be remembered. The healing has always been in how you deal with the memories and where they fit into your life today.

I can't tell you how many times I admired you from afar. I marveled at your ability to reveal your wounded self. Most adults molested as children or sexually abused children never find the strength or courage to break their silence or face the past. You are the example of a wounded healer. In so many ways, you have been my teacher, and for that I am eternally grateful. Until we meet in heaven.

  Love,
  Mom

Hear the Cry
of People
Suffering

I have observed the misery of my people who are in Egypt;
I have heard their cry on account of their taskmasters.
Indeed, I know their sufferings,
and I have come down to deliver them from the Egyptians,
and to bring them up out of that land
to a good and broad land,
a land flowing with milk and honey.
—Exodus 3:7-8

Judas the Betrayer

For the prayer corner: Three dimes.

Then Satan entered into Judas called Iscariot, who was one of the twelve; he went away and conferred with the chief priests and officers of the temple police about how he might betray him to them. They were greatly pleased and agreed to give him money. So he consented and began to look for an opportunity to betray him to them when no crowd was present. (Luke 22:3-6)

Read Luke 22:1-53.

Judas Iscariot, one of the chosen, was accustomed to having money in his hand. He kept records of the disciple's money and made the purchases for the group. It is ironic that his reputation convinced others of his trustworthiness. Indeed, his weakness for love of money caused his life to end in disgrace. For thirty pieces of silver this traitor led the Roman soldiers and Temple police, armed with torches and weapons, to the Garden of Gethsemane. There the traitor greeted the Master with a kiss. Then he followed the soldiers as they bound Jesus and led him away.

Mr. Soto convinced his fellow teachers that he also was trustworthy. As a dedicated teacher, he often helped his students after class. He showed youthful enthusiasm, snappy clothing, and good looks, and several of the eighth-grade girls had crushes on him. No one suspected he needed to be close to young girls in order to feel more in control and better about his life.

When girls came into his office to pick up their weekly progress reports, he carefully examined their changing bodies. It never crossed these girls' minds that in walking though the door, they were in dangerous territory. Mr. Soto let himself be governed by this dominating passion, rather than conquering it with therapy.

School was intended to be a place where children were safe from these kinds of people, not a place where their innocence was betrayed by a trusted person in authority. Unfortunately, three teachers in this district had been charged with sexual misconduct with a minor. Parents were outraged. The local police began working with child protective services, and together they implemented a sexual abuse prevention program at every school in the district.

One Friday afternoon when Mr. Soto took his homeroom class into the assembly, he was surprised to see several police and professional people present. He became more uncomfortable as the representatives from the various services presented examples of sexual abuse. They were describing some of the things he had tricked his students into doing behind the closed door of his office. He was guilty of rubbing a girl on her back, then resting his hand on the bra strap. Then his face turned scarlet red when the professionals suggested a child molester might offer to take pictures of children in skimpy bathing suits and tell them he was entering them in a beauty contest.

Mr. Soto worried that if he walked out of the assembly, he would look suspicious. He hoped against hope that this was another "education program" and the girls would not see the truth through their puppy-love eyes. Mr. Soto was wrong. At the end of the presentation, some of them stayed in the gym instead of returning to their last class of the day.

Each girl told a similar story to officers about Mr. Soto's conduct. The police believed the girls were telling the truth. At the end of the school day, Mr. Soto was taken in by the police for questioning. At the police station, he denied the stories. He even questioned the police, asking, "How could intelligent men of blue accept the word of a mere child against that of a professional like myself?" He added, "I have an excellent reputation as a teacher and in this community. This must be a mistake."

The police read him his rights and suggested he call a lawyer.

The Denial

In the book *When Your Child Has Been Molested*, several reasons are given for denial when the abuser is approached by the arresting officer.[4] Think of all the person stands to lose if the victim's story is believed.

- Rejection by immediate and extended family is likely.
- Professional standing and employment are in jeopardy.
- If found guilty of criminal sexual conduct, probation and prison is assured.

Many abusers are so ashamed of their behavior, they can't admit it. For some, their shame forces them to continue to deny, even when there is overwhelming evidence of their guilt.

Many abusers have character disorders that allow them to lie convincingly and persistently for months or even years in an attempt to convince others of their innocence.

Responding to the Sex Offender

Statistics tell us most child molesters are people whom our children know and trust. With this in mind, a parent often will have a basic relationship with the abuser. Especially if it is a case of generational sexual abuse or incest, an ongoing relationship is possible.

Sex offenders need to know:
- Sexual abuse is sexual activity exploiting a child who is not capable of understanding or resisting coercion (threats, offers of gifts, and so on). Sexual activity may range from exhibitionism to

113

fondling to intercourse. Rape, child molestation, and incest are all forms of sexual abuse.

• Persons who sexually assault others are breaking the law, and criminal charges can be filed against them because the behavior they choose is illegal. Sex offenders must be told that such behavior must stop. Beware of promises that "it will never happen again." Parents who choose to believe such a promise are putting their child at great risk.

• Sex offenders must be told they need professional help. Far too often offenders do not seek the therapy they require. If criminal charges are not filed because certain criteria are not met (not necessarily because the abuse did not take place), many offenders simply are not forced to get assistance. Help is available, but sadly enough, if it doesn't come from the directive of a judge, often the offenders continues to deny that they have a problem.[5]

Criteria for Criminal Charges

For criminal charges to be filed in King County, Seattle, Washington, a child must be able to:

• Describe a sexual act in enough detail and specificity to establish clearly that a crime occurred.

• Convince a number of competent professionals that the child is telling the truth.

• Meet the legal standards for being a competent witness.

• Appear able to say it in an open courtroom in front of the accused and withstand direct and cross-examination.

About half the cases reviewed each year by the special assault unit of the King County Prosecuting Attorney's office do not result in the filing of charges, because these criteria are not met, not necessarily because the abuse did not take place.[6]

The Rights of the Sex Offender

It is rare for children to make false accusations. Dr. David Jones, of the highly respected Kempe Center for the Prevention and

114

Treatment of Child Abuse and Neglect, recently conducted a study reviewing referrals of sexual abuse reported to the Denver Social Service Department. The study found that only a small fraction of cases were determined to be fictitious: in only 1.5 percent were the children thought to be lying.

- Persons accused of crimes have constitutional rights to:

1. Have a lawyer.
2. Know all the evidence against them.
3. Have a public trial.
4. Make the state prove beyond a reasonable doubt that the crime occurred.

The new state law affecting these cases—the child sexual abuse hearsay exception—does not allow a person to be convicted of child molestation based only on someone else's statement. If a child is too young or too traumatized to testify in court, the case can proceed only where there is independent corroboration of the crime and a judge determines that the child's statements meet stringent standards for reliability.

The defense attorney is professionally required to defend the client just as vigorously when it is obvious that the child is telling the truth as when the client is innocent. A defense attorney's principal concern in a criminal trial is not for the truth but to obtain an acquittal, no matter how incompatible with the truth that may be.

Simply because a child makes a statement does not mean that someone will be charged with a crime and go to jail. In every case, there is careful assessment by a number of professionals to ensure preservation of all legal safeguards for the person accused of crimes, rightly or wrongly.[7]

* * *

From a Sex Offender to His Victim[8]

Dear Julia:

There is something that's been on my mind and heavy in my heart, but I didn't know what to do about it. Soon after they charged me with my crime, I began to realize the real impact of what I had done. I have been trying very hard for the last four years to change myself and to understand others so that my life can be different and I can come out of here a better person, husband, son, brother, and for you, a real father. That's why I'm in a special program to get help.

I finally realized that I, alone, am responsible for all my own choices and actions. I know now the extent of my obligations—to myself, my family, and to the society in which I live.

I wonder a lot about how come I missed knowing all this before coming to prison. I worked hard before coming to prison and have worked hard in here. I get 25 cents an hour for the work I do, and some of the jobs pay 90 cents per hour. That's a real joke for me—after all those things we used to buy and play with. I miss all the times we shopped and I could surprise you with neat things. Everything seems so bad, but the most important thing for you to remember is—I know we loved each other and I could have made it back after going broke.

Things weren't good, but it wasn't the end of the world, like your mom felt about it—but then she always gets stressed out and worse since her accident and feelings of pressure. But you girls did everything for her, to help out around the house and with the boys. My God, what more could she have asked for? All of us were so close. That's what kept me going. I still get a warm tingle when I wake up in the morning and think about you girls crawling in to cuddle with me. It was so hard for me to separate why loving you so much could put me in prison and leave you, and for me to be so alone here. Everyone here hates me and treats me like dirt. They call me "baby raper." That's not me. For a long time I told myself I was only guilty for loving too much.

Now I've had to face how I feel as different from what I think, and to make decisions about my behavior. I know

now I can't live based on what just feels good at the time. That is what I used to do—telling myself if it feels good it must be okay, 'cause I wasn't hurting anyone. I even convinced myself I wasn't hurting you, 'cause whenever you said it burned or hurt, I wouldn't push myself on you to go beyond our exchanges of back rubs and hugs and love.

No one can ever say what happened was because I was on drugs or drunk. I never did drugs and didn't even smoke. Now I know it was just me. I was the adult. It wasn't your fault, even though you came to my bed—you both, in your own individual ways, wanted to be near me. You never pushed me away. We laughed and played all kinds of ways—rubbing and kissing—and I loved it too. Not all the guys in here understand the relationship we had. Theirs was different. I know I could never take a chance to hurt you and your future relationships. Now I can only hope I haven't.

I have learned there's lots of "what if" something different had happened or been said—like what if your mom had said it would be better for us all to get out of bed at the same time, instead of just getting mad when you girls would get in bed with me. When she knew I was feeling around, she'd go off mad again. What if we could have talked about her feelings about her dad dying last year . . . or her jealousy about you girls being thin and her gaining weight . . . all those things she'd get mad about. And, I'd stuff my feelings too.

I'm sorry. They tell me in this program that saying "I'm sorry" isn't enough. But I'm really sorry for all of it. You are not to blame for anything I did or your mom did. You have your life ahead of you. A new word is helping me feel a little better. The new word I learned is *restitution*, and it means I want to be sure you can talk to someone—like a counselor—so you won't blame yourself for what happened and for me coming to prison . . . and I want to pay for you to talk

117

to a counselor. That is how I have learned to deal with my feelings and problems—especially when I think about what I did to you.

I guess I can't expect or even ask you to forgive me, or even to understand. I am making changes and can only hope someday that you will be able to see the changes in me. I believe you can change, too, in the way you think about what I did. I pray God to make everything better for you.

I am sorry, Julia. I still love you—but in a different way.

Dad

* * *

Prayer for a Sex Offender

There are so many of them, Lord. They use their eyes to search out children to exploit. They use their hands to touch and teach things that were meant to be kept in and for the sanctity of marriage. They use their mouths to promise enticing gifts, to weave a web of fear and intimidation, trapping their victims for years in silent pain and suffering.

O God, open their eyes to the damage they have done. Help them to acknowledge their responsibility for the sins of sexual violence they have committed, that they may mourn their actions.

O God, touch their minds. Take the distortions, the illusions, the twisted beliefs, the deviant fantasies, and the confusion, and bring a new vision to them that they will discover the sexuality God intended for them.

O God, we pray for the sex offenders who are seeking treatment. By their actions alone, they are making the world a safer place for our children. Please provide skilled and caring people who can lead them without judgment and offer hope for their future.

O God, we pray for those offenders who are troubled by guilt, fear, sadness, anger, and remorse, that they may be comforted.

O God, we pray for those who are abandoned and rejected by their families and their churches, forgotten in prisons, that they may be delivered from their loneliness.

O God, we pray for those who are accused by false witnesses and condemned to prison terms, that justice may be served.

O God, we pray for the sex offenders in prison, hated, ridiculed, taunted, abused, raped, and their very lives threatened by other prisoners. Give them courage, treatment, and your protection in the healing process.

O God, we pray for those who carry the burden of sins and are afraid to ask forgiveness and face the consequences, that they may turn toward you to begin the path of reconciliation and healing.

O God, we pray your blessing on all sex offenders, because we know that in your heart all people have equal access to your love and acceptance. Help us to love as you love, and to live as you intend us to live.

By your own sufferings, Lord, heal the wounds in the hearts of all sex offenders, especially (name of the person who abused your child). Amen.

TWENTY-FIFTH DAY

Tamar,
Victim with a Voice

For the prayer corner: A torn doll's dress or cloth.

*Then Amnon said to Tamar, "Bring the food into the chamber, so
that I may eat from your hand." So Tamar took the cakes she
had made, and brought them into the chamber to Amnon her
brother. But when she brought them near him to eat, he took
hold of her, and said to her, "Come, lie with me, my sister."*

*She answered him, "No, my brother, do not force me; for such
a thing is not done in Israel; do not do anything so vile!"*

(2 Samuel 13:10-11)

Read 2 Samuel 13:1-22.

Mandy, a Sunday school teacher, spread her study books on the
dining room table. She started to prepare her lesson on the feud
between David's sons, Absalom and Amnon. Mandy was familiar
with the story of David, his defeats and his victories. She knew he
committed adultery with Bathsheba. She didn't know anything

120

about his children. Her eyes widened as she read about the rape of Tamar, David's only daughter. Mandy, a churchgoer, never remembered a pastor using this text for a sermon.

Then in reviewing her Sunday school lesson, she noticed a glaring omission. The writer didn't even acknowledge the violation against Tamar. It was as if the rape was lifted out of the story. Mandy was troubled as to why her church paper omitted the rape. Maybe they felt as she did about her own rape. She wanted to hide the fact that her half brother took her virginity. Mandy read on with interest. Tamar was a fellow sister, a kinswoman of terror.

The words Amnon "grabbed" (NIV) Tamar glared off the page. For a moment Mandy's hands trembled as she remembered. She stood paralyzed in a time frame that felt like the event was happening again.

She spoke aloud, "No. No. You can't do this to me! Bob, I'm your sister. It isn't right! I'm a virgin! Please don't! Please!"

Mandy's tense body went weak. Resting her head on the brown leather Bible as the tears trickled down her cheeks, she cried out, "Why didn't he listen to me? Why didn't my parents help me instead of saying I must have been exaggerating? Why did they tell me they didn't want to hear another word about it ever again?" The pain of rejection and self-blame heaved her body.

Frequently, as in the story of Mandy and many other victims of incestuous rape, a parent is aware of the family voilence. Tragically for all concerned, they rarely come to the aid of the victim. Scripture says that King David was angry, but he does not directly denounce the crime committed against her. Instead, verse 21 reveals why Tamar's father chose the actions he did: "He would not punish his son Amnon, because he loved him, for he was firstborn.

"David's anger signifies complete sympathy for Amnon and total disregard for Tamar. How appropriate that the story never refers to David and Tamar as father and daughter! The father identifies with the son; the adulterer supports the rapist; male has joined male to deny justice for the female."[9]

Tamar, like other victims violated in their family circle, remained outside the structure of family relationships. Amnon's sins of lust sparked a flame that ignited a forest fire of hatred toward Tamar. "Then Amnon was seized with a very great loathing for her; indeed, his loathing was even greater than the lust he had felt for her" (13:15).

Amnon's dismissal is a lifelong sentence of desolation for this virgin-stripped child. Though child she may have been, she claims her voice: "No, my brother; for this wrong in sending me away is greater than the other that you did to me" (13:16).

Amnon uses his authority against the protesting girl, with parting words (from Hebrew): "Send *this* away." "For Amnon, Tamar is a thing, 'this' he wants thrown out. She is trash."[10] His words knife deeply into the heart of her awakening sexual center.

Tamar partly reveals her pain by tearing her long-sleeved robe, which is supposed to show that she is a virgin daughter of the king. "Sadly, what that robe proclaims, Tamar is no longer. . . . Tamar is a victim of shame that her clothes cannot hide."[11]

Their Voices Must Be Heard

We must break the silence concerning rape, incest, and other acts of sexual violence against innocent victims. Today ten, twenty, fifty years after the fact, courageous men and women, many of them Christians, are starting to break their silence. They are beginning to tell their stories about the sexual abuse they experienced as children. Their voices must be heard. Their pain must be shared. Healing must begin so that:

1. Others will have hope for recovery.

2. Others may be given help.

3. Others will protect children.

4. People will understand, not necessarily make allowances, but understand the impact of sexual abuse.

5. Victims can become survivors and receive affirmation of their personhood.

6. Survivors can break the power of the secret they carried for the family.

7. Survivors can claim what happened to them openly as part of their history.

8. Survivors can give the shame and guilt they carried back to the perpetrator whose responsibility it really is.

9. Survivors can find others who have had similar experiences and discover the common consequences of sexual abuse.

10. Survivors can quit vacillating between believing and not believing that the abuse happened to them.

11. Survivors can understand their sexuality and how they have been affected by the abuse.

12. Survivors can feel fully loved by God and fully loved by themselves.

13. Survivors can open up the possibility of the abuser finding healing through confession, asking for forgiveness, and seeking appropriate group and individual therapy.[12]

Crazy

By Martha Janssen[13]

This is crazy
I am crying
    screaming
    hiding my face in shame.
I am weak
    and can't rest.
My stomach is like a stone
    and my fingers ache from clenching.
I suffer.
You!
You walk calmly
    among people, relatives.
They don't know you
    as I do.
You smile
    and feel no guilt
    no shame.
You walk away from my pain.
This is crazy.
I carry the weight of the sentence
    but you are the killer.

* * *

From a Victim to His Victimizer[14]

There's no way you can know how much rage and anger I have felt about what you did to me—and here I am in prison. It isn't fair that I am here because of what you did to me and you are out there going free, like nothing ever happened. Just because I was a coward and couldn't tell anybody. I feel lousy about that, too. Who would have believed a kid? I was just a little boy. No one was there for me.

It wasn't my fault that Dad wasn't home. When I asked him to stay home with us more, he told me he had to pay so many bills and that's why he had to work so much and be gone so much, and drink so much. But he loved us. Sometimes he tried to fix buddy's bike, but he just didn't know how. I keep wondering if he would have told me some more about sex—if I hadn't told him that was old stuff to me . . . if I hadn't laughted at him when he started to tell me about how little yellow hairs would grow in my palms if I touched myself and played with it, you know . . . down there. He acted like he didn't know about you showing me all about sex.

Sure, like you said, now I know it all, but I thought that was supposed to make me a better lover. And the first girl I told about you—well, she got sick at her stomach, so I didn't tell anyone else, and I've never asked to have sex with a girl again.

Here in prison, I take it whenever I want it, from whoever and whatever way I want it. I'm trying to figure out why I do that. Well, I've got a bunch of years here to figure it out. I've always wondered if you knew what we did was really a "crime." I've wondered too what would have happened if I had told someone about what you did to me. They probably wouldn't have believed me, you being a Sunday school teacher and all that. I guess that's another thing that makes me angry. Everybody thinks you're such a good person. If they only knew.

There is a real treatment program in here that I've just gotten started in. And the chaplain has gotten me to come to a Bible study group. Both my therapist and the chaplain tell us we need to work on becoming able to forgive the person who abused us. Yah, I'm not the only one who was abused. I'm trying to deal with my anger and hate about what happened. I have tried to pray that you will yet talk to someone about how you took advantage of me, and maybe someday tell people you aren't as good as they thought. Be honest with yourself. That's what they tell me. I can tell you that it sounds good to be able to be free from all this hate.

I wanted to write and tell you that I'm working at being able to forgive you. I'm not there, yet. I pray to God that I'll make it someday.

Ned

* * *

Absalom the Advocate

Absalom could not reverse what had happened to Tamar, but he did not hesitate to use his power on behalf of his sister. He became her advocate. All victims of sexual violence need the support of others, whether we know their names or not. Below are some suggestions on how to be an advocate for victims and survivors of sexual abuse.

- Check with your community, church, and school librarians for books on incest and sexual abuse for both adults and children. Request important additions on the topic.

- Write to newspapers. Respond to reports of incest and sexual abuse and give your support to family treatment programs for families and offenders amenable to treatment.

- Write letters of support to prosecutors, judges, and child protective services to exert their influence and power to obtain amenable treatment for offenders, and treatment programs for families who have experienced incest.

• Lobby your legislators for appropriate legislation to promote rehabilitation for incest offenders amenable to treatment.

• Encourage your YWCA or YMCA to develop women's and men's support centers. Become active in your center.

• Present a resolution in your church and church conference that addresses the problem of sexual abuse, whether within or without the family.

• Volunteer membership in a conference domestic violence task force to assist your conference's commitment to work on related problems of family violence.[15]

Memories

My friend said,
  "When I was little I think *IT* happened to me."
And I thought,
  What exactly was *IT?*
  "Was it touching here?"
  "Was it touching there?"
  "Or was it the *awful touch?*"

I know my friend is not alone.
  There are hundreds of thousands of them,
  their innocence ripped out
  like wolves feeding on wounded lambs.
They are torn and bleeding.
  Huddled in corners of shame.
  Too petrified to move.
  Too terrified to ask for help.
  Too guilt-ridden to tell anyone.

The memories are buried with the pain.
Yet flames flicker under molten ashes as silent tears fall.

Prayer for a Victim of Sexual Abuse

O God, help my friend in the difficulties of life. Open his or her eyes to see the truth. To have courage to remember instead of trying to forget. To feel what he has experienced instead of repressing it.

My friend is afraid to tell even you this awful secret. He doesn't know yet that you are the kind of friend who doesn't blame him for things he did in secret places. Most of all, God, please help my friend get to know you better so you can be his very best Friend. Amen.

Christian Response to Child Sexual Abuse

Whoever welcomes one such child in my name welcomes me.
If any of you put a stumbling block
before one of these little ones who believe in me,
it would be better for you
if a great millstone were fastened around your neck
and you were drowned in the depth of the sea.
—Matthew 18:5-6

TWENTY-SIXTH DAY

Whose Sin Is This?

For the prayer corner:
One black paper heart and one white paper heart.

The righteousness of God [is] through faith in Jesus Christ for all who believe. For there is no distinction, since all have sinned and fall short of the glory of God. (Romans 3:22-23)

Jackie lived in the projects and counted the days to Sunday when the Son Shine bus arrived to take the waiting children to Sunday school. She always left church with a warm feeling which carried over for most of the week at home. When Pastor Tom told her she could get a scholarship for Junior High Church Camp, she went home and packed her bag.

Camp was everything Jackie dreamed of and more. She especially liked the extra attention she got from the pastor. Sometimes they would go to their special spot near Slide Rock. Large boulders loomed up on both sides and Pastor Tom called it the stone house.

The pastor's wife, Bonnie, liked camp, too. One afternoon while walking the canyon trail she glanced down at the jagged

131

boulders and layered waterfalls below. To her shock, she saw her husband and Jackie with some of their clothes off. She immediately ran back to the lodge and called Jackie's mother, demanding that she drive up to camp "tonight" and get her "little whore daughter."

Bonnie did what many people do. She gave the sin of sexual violence to Jackie, the victim. Maybe, she thought, because Jackie wore shorts and a tank top, she enticed her husband. Or perhaps Jackie was already sexually active with boys and she was just teasing her husband, who couldn't help himself. Obviously, Bonnie reasoned, if Jackie was behaving like a good Christian, she never would have started such sinful behavior. Bonnie, like many adults, believed the myth that children provoke sexual abuse by their seductive or attention-seeking behaviors.

Jackie returned home carrying the burden of shame and feeling like the worst sinner in the world. She never returned to Sunday school.

Bonnie in her ignorance was unable to name the sin accurately and place the responsibility where it belonged on her husband—the child molester. Jackie carried unfairly Pastor Tom's sin of sexual violence.

The Sin of Sexual Violence

• *It is a bodily sin.* Jackie sought attention from Pastor Tom, not abuse. He caused psychological injury to Jackie when he molested her. Any form of sexual coercion or violence violates the bodily integrity of another person.

• *It is a relational sin.* Jackie trusted the pastor not to betray or intentionally injure her. Pastor Tom took advantage of her vulnerability. When a violation of trust in a relation occurs, it destroys the possibility of relationship between people.

• *It is a social sin.* Jackie was raised in a society that told her to obey adults and to do what they say. Pastor Tom was seen as a powerful authority figure. This sin thrives in an environment of sexism which sustains subordinate/dominant relationships and encourages or silently condones individual acts of sexual violence, creating a hostile environment particularly for women and children.

- *It is a sin against sexuality.* It is not a sin *because* it is sexual; instead, sexual violence is the distortion and misuse of sexuality, and thus a sin against sexuality, part of God's good creation.

The Just Response to the Sin

- The first response of justice to the sins of sexual violence is *righteous anger.*

- The second response of justice is *compassion for the victim.*

- The third response of justice is *advocacy for the victim.*

- The fourth response of justice is *holding the offender legally and spiritually accountable for his/her sin against the victim and the community.*

- The fifth response of justice is *prevention*; addressing the roots (sexism, child abuse, sexual ethics, economics) and not merely the symptoms of sexual violence.[16]

Let Me Be Your Justice, Lord

O God, help me to appreciate and channel my anger into directions that can bring healing and wholeness to the larger community of victims of sexual abuse. Lord, use my righteous anger to work for peace and justice.

Oh God, sometimes a judgmental spirit comes over me and I fail to realize what it must feel like to walk in the shoes of an offender or a survivor of sexual abuse. Open my critical eyes to see as you do that I may love as you love. Touch my body, my hands, and my mouth with a holy compassion that I may bring understanding to others.

Oh God, sometimes the pain is so great that I do nothing to make right the wrongs done to innocent people. Help me to remember that one person doing one thing for the kingdom can make a difference. I ask you to give me the strength and fill me with the desire to work as an advocate.

133

O God, this world you put us in does not seem fair sometimes. The sins of our fathers and mothers visit the second and third generation with no hope of stopping. Laws are made to be broken, and courts find the guilty innocent on a technicality. It just doesn't make sense. The only thing that does make sense is to keep speaking out that those who commit crimes against God's laws and society's must pay for their acts of disobedience. *Justice must be served against innocent victims.*

O God, you made a perfect world for us. With your hand you created the first man and woman. You blessed them with children. In your eyes each and every human is equal and lovingly respected by you. But something happened in your world. Men, women, and children are caught in the oppression of sexism and are strangely silent about sexual matters. This is a breeding ground for sex offenders to prey on unsuspecting victims. Help me to work to broaden the attitudes of others that they may understand the roots of sexual violence. *Amen.*

Come to the Wounded Healer

A Sermon on Sexual Abuse, by David W. Mann[17]

For the prayer corner: A small cross or crucifix.

Today we're beginning our annual series Festival of the Family. We want to look at issues related to family life and how we can renew, strengthen, and minister to our families.

The title for my message is "Come to the Wounded Healer." I'd like to read again from Isaiah 53, verses 4 and 5.

Surely he took up our infirmities and carried our sorrows,
yet we considered him stricken by God,
*   smitten by him, and afflicted.*
But he was pierced for our transgressions
*   he was crushed for our iniquities;*
the punishment that brought us peace was upon him,
*   and by his wounds we are healed. (NIV)*

135

Jesus suffered on the cross, not only for our sins and transgressions, but he also suffered for our infirmities. In the fourth verse Isaiah says, "Surely he took up [or has borne] our infirmities and carried our sorrow." The Amplified Version says, "Surely he has borne our griefs, sicknesses, weakness, and distress, and carried our sorrows and pain." Another translation says, "And carried our torments." This refers to something in addition to our sins and iniquities that Jesus bore on the cross. The crucified Jesus also bore those wounds in our lives. Those wounds that have left deep and lasting scars, that have continued to bring brokenness and pain in our lives.

A naturalist, by looking at a cross section of a tree that is cut down, can examine the rings in the tree and tell you the history of that tree's development. He can point to a certain ring on the tree and say, "This year was a year of drought. In this year the tree was struck by lightning. This year was a good year. There was plenty of rain, perhaps even too much rain. This year was a year of blight and disease." Hidden under the bark of the tree is the story of what has happened through the years of the development of that tree.

And so it is for many persons. For some of you here this morning, hidden under the outside surface are rings of wounds. Rings of wounds that have been with you in your life, that are part of who you are and what has happened in your life. Scars. Secrets. Hidden secrets. Secrets that you've dared not tell to another living soul, because they are too painful to tell.

It might have been a frightening episode of being locked in a closet for punishment. It may have been that years ago a brother, an uncle, or your father introduced a little girl to the mysteries, no, to the *miseries* of sex, out behind the barn or in the house when everybody was gone. It may have been an abusive parent, or another adult who wounded you verbally, physically, or sexually, and it has left rings of thoughts, and feelings, and pain that have stayed there in your life. They have been implanted deep within your being.

Perhaps it is the kind of secret you have never told anyone. Or perhaps you tried to tell people, but they didn't want to hear it. They didn't want to listen. You may have been afraid to tell what happened to you for fear they wouldn't believe you. Or for fear they would say that you're the one who was bad rather than the one who inflicted this on you.

And so you carried that wound, you carried that pain all your life. And it continues to deeply affect your feeling about yourself, your feeling about life, the fears that you live with, the relationships that you have.

It is a wound that has never been healed. What I want to tell you is that if you're carrying a painful secret wound in your life, Jesus suffered for that wound. Jesus suffered for those infirmities, and he wants to bring healing and release into your life. The Holy Spirit will bring a special healing into our lives, beyond the simplicity of saying a prayer and reading the Scriptures.

Romans 8:26 says, "Likewise the Spirit helps us in our weakness [KJV: infirmities]; for we do not know how to pray as we ought, but that very Spirit intercedes [for us] with sighs too deep for words," or "with groans that words cannot express" (NIV).

This morning I want to talk about coming to the Wounded Healer and experiencing healing for that deep and secret wound you may have carried throughout your life. I want to talk particularly today about a subject most of us don't want to hear about, but it's one that we dare not close our eyes and ears to. Some of you may be uncomfortable, and I understand that. Some of you may wish that your children could exit at this point, but your children need to be here. And your children need to hear what I feel I have been asked to say this morning.

I want to talk about sexual abuse. I want to talk about physical abuse. I want to talk about wives who are abused—physically, verbally, emotionally. We'd like to believe that these things happen out in the world, but not in the church. Certainly not in a Mennonite church. And certainly, most certainly, not in our church. But I am aware of secret and terrible pain that exists in persons' lives within the Mennonite church and within our congregation. I am convinced there are wounds in people's lives here that I know nothing about, and that nobody else knows about, except just you. And you've carried that pain, you've carried that wound all your life.

These are the grim statistics. Two out of four girls and one in seven boys are sexually abused before they are eighteen years old. Ninety percent of the time the abuse is inflicted by a person they know, not by a stranger. Fifty percent of the time it is by somebody within their own family—a brother, a father, an uncle, a cousin, a grandparent, someone who took advantage of a natural bridge of trust to violate another person's life. That is called incest. One out of six females are victims of incest. It is reported that on the campus at Arizona State University, one out of four girls on the campus has experienced date rape.

From my personal awareness, from talking to other pastors and counselors, I know that we in the Mennonite church are not very different from the general population in those statistics.

Now I recognize that that's shocking, and I recognize some of you are probably getting the urge to get up and leave right now, because you'd rather not hear the rest of what I have to say. If we just didn't have to know it, maybe it would go away. But I risk talking about this because there may be children and adults here who are carrying a horrendous secret that they don't know what to do with, that they don't know who to talk to about. Some of you may have been carrying such a secret for decades and decades, and it's been devastating to your lives. It's been devastating to your relationships. I want you to know, I want to say it again, Jesus suffered for that wound. Jesus felt the pain of that infirmity, that torment. He died because he cares about that pain you have or are experiencing, and he wants to bring healing and a release to you. Notice in the last part of the fifth verse it says, "And by his wounds we are healed."

The problem is real and it has left deep scars on many lives. Many of you read in the September issue of the *Gospel Herald* last year the article simply entitled "The Tree."[18] It was the story of a woman, a grown woman now, who was repeatedly violated by her father from the age of four until her early twenties. As a young girl, she became pregnant by her father, who then took her out to the barn, where he performed an abortion. He continued to violate her into her early twenties. She tried to tell her mother, and her mother didn't want to hear it . She tried to tell her pastor, and her pastor didn't want to deal with it. Nobody wanted to deal with it. Nobody wanted to listen to her pain.

Years later she began to find healing because of the love and tenderness of her husband and of a small group who loved her enough to listen to the pain and help her through the beginning process of healing in her life. They helped her find release from that dreadful secret, to experience forgiveness. Not only to experience forgiveness in *her* life, but to find the ability to *give* forgiveness. The deep desire of her heart has become to find healing for her family. I just learned last night that this dear sister's father died recently, and the family—who doesn't want to hear what happened—have rejected and ostracized her from the family because they don't want to listen. They don't want to know. Thank God there are brothers and sisters in the church who are listening and who are helping her to find healing.

Some of you here know what I am talking about because you have carried these wounds. I don't know who you are, and I don't know what those wounds are. But some of you I know have found healing from the Wounded Healer, who has brought wholeness back into your life. Yet some of you are still carrying an unspoken, dreadful secret in your life that is leaving a profound effect on you.

There is altogether the possibility that in this audience there may be persons who are abusers. And I want you to know that there is also healing from the Wounded Healer for those who are abusers as well as those who are abused. There is healing for you in Jesus.

And again, in Roman 8:26, Paul says that the Spirit of God helps our infirmities. He helps our weakness with prayers. The Spirit makes intercession for us with groanings that can't be uttered. And when Paul says that the Spirit helps us, he means that the Spirit becomes our partner in healing. Our helper in healing. He works along with us in mutual participation in the healing. I need to say that healing from this kind of wound is not simply a zap from heaven. It is something that the Wounded Healer, along with your willingness to enter into that healing process, can and will work together to bring you to wholeness.

In closing, let me share several suggestions that may be helpful to you. Number one, the point I'm trying to make is that if you have a dreadful secret in your life, one of the first important things you can do, one of the greatest resources you have for experiencing healing, is to allow another human person to share that pain with you. There are many people who love you. There are many people who will understand. Yes, there may be some who don't want to hear and who don't understand, but there are many who will.

If you have a dreadful secret you have been hiding all your life, I want to ask you, urge you, to go to someone. Come to me, your pastor, to the associate pastor, one of the elders, or to someone you choose. Let someone help carry that burden and help you find the healing that God brings.

I say to any children who are here, *if* somebody has been touching you in inappropriate ways and in inappropriate places that have made you feel uncomfortable, you need to tell somebody. If you can't tell a parent, tell your Sunday school teacher. Tell another adult you trust. The number one resource is another person who can hear and love and share and help you begin your healing process.

Now the most important thing I have to say is the invitation to come to the Wounded Healer. Come to Jesus who bore your infirmities and carried your sorrows and torments. Every pain you have felt, he has felt. He has borne that with you. The Wounded Healer wants to bring healing into your life. "Surely he took up our infirmities and carried our sorrows . . . and by his wounds we [can be] healed."

The Healing Will Be a Process

Where can you begin? How can you begin this healing process? In many cases of this kind of wound in your life, the healing will not be instantaneous. They are deep wounds, long-standing pain with profound effects. Healing will be a process, rather than an event. But an event may be the beginning.

1. *You need to face your problem squarely.* One of the first steps in experiencing healing for your brokenness is to open the closet door where you've tried to hide that hurt from yourself and from others. Acknowledge the wound to yourself and to another human being. James 5:16 says, "Confess your sins [KJV: faults] to

one another, and pray for one another, so that you may be healed."
You need to allow another person to enter in with you in your
healing process, in coming before the Wounded Healer who can
bring healing and wholeness.

2. *Accept your responsibility in the matter.* You are saying,
"Wait a minute, wait a minute, I am the victim. I'm the one who
has been violated." Yes, that's true, but what responsibility do you
have for the hate and resentment you have hung onto in your life?
For the patterns of escape and avoidance and hiding you have
used to try to cope with this pain rather than to come forward and
deal with it?

If you are here this morning and may be an abuser, the one who
caused the abuse, part of accepting responsibility is to quit blaming other people for what you do and quit making excuses for
why you did it. There are tons of excuses given by abusers to justify, to rationalize what they do. Come for forgiveness and come for
restoration.

3. *Ask yourself if you really want to be healed.* Do you remember when Jesus came to the pool of Siloam, to the man who had
lain there for thirty-two years with a crippling condition? Jesus
asked him a strange question: "Do you want to get well?" And you
say, "Why even ask that?" I'll tell you why. Because sometimes carrying the pain meets a need in your life. You may feel justified in
hanging onto that resentment. You may use it as a crutch. You
may use it as an excuse, and thereby avoid responsibility for
change. So do you want to be healed? Do you want to be healed
enough to open the door to that secret closet and let another
brother or sister walk with you and help you find your way to the
Wounded Healer? Or are you content to live with the fear, the
hurt and anger and resentment that is destroying your life? You
have a choice to either continue to live with it or to come for healing.

4. *If you are going to experience healing, you need to ask for
grace to forgive everybody involved in the problem.* I know that's
difficult, very difficult, but with the help of Jesus you can be released from the anger and pain and will be able to forgive others,

to release them from the desire for revenge or justice. An unforgiving spirit will not only block your healing. It will also block growth in your spiritual life.

5. *You need to forgive yourself.* Sometimes when we feel so devastated, it's hard for us to believe anybody could love us, that anybody could accept us or forgive us or embrace us—most of all, God. When working with persons who have been abused, we sometimes assume they will understand that the abuser is the perpetrator and they, the victims, are not responsible. But it doesn't always work that way. For instance, a woman who has been raped will often struggle with a sense of guilt that she somehow caused or deserved this. Part of the pain comes from her blaming herself. Our court system often adds to that pain by pointing blame to the victim. God loves us *unconditionally* no matter what has happened in our lives. There is no one unworthy to be loved and forgiven by God. He loves you unconditionally. When God forgives you, he buries it in the deepest sea. He doesn't remember it anymore. Sometimes the hardest thing in the world is to forgive ourselves.

6. *Ask the Holy Spirit to show you your real problem.* What is the blockage in your life? He can teach you how you can pray in a way that will begin to make a difference in your life and the lives of others as well. Remember again Romans 8:26: "The Holy Spirit helps us with our infirmities." He helps us by praying in us and through us and for us. He is there to be the agent of God's healing.

To Pastors Everywhere

The tragedy of sexual abuse is one of those things we would rather not talk about or deal with, and yet it is a reality confronting us in the church as well as in our communities today.

Although you may find it difficult to address this topic in a Sunday morning message, I would encourage you to be bold in opening a door of hope for those persons in your congregation who are hurting from sexual abuse. Most often they have been hiding this dreadful secret for a long time and are uncertain anyone would

142

care enough or be understanding enough to be a safe place to share their deep wound and begin to find healing.

According to statistics, one in three girls and one in seven boys will be sexually assaulted before they are eighteen years old. One in six females is a victim of incest. Don't be fooled into thinking these figures are not true in your church. Just over a year ago I preached a message on sexual abuse and how to begin the healing process. At this time I have become aware of eighteen persons, both male and female, who have been sexually violated.

When you show your willingness to talk about this issue in public, you will find persons gathering courage and hope to come to you or to other caring persons to find understanding, support, and healing.

Sometimes we pastors have been silent because we are afraid to address such a sensitive and controversial topic. Other times pastors have focused their energies on a redemptive ministry to the offender at the expense of the victim. Or we may mistakenly give a simplistic admonition to the victim: "Just forgive the offender and get on with your life." We do that rather than deal with the offender and the brokenness in a way that will allow for true healing for both the victim and the offender. Healing is a long, slow process but one that is possible with the support of a loving Christian community and the healing power of the Holy Spirit. Many times the victim will also need the help of a counselor skilled in the area of sexual abuse.

Take courage. Sound a note of hope for those in your flock who may be carrying a lifelong wound that continues to bring havoc into their personal relationship and their spiritual development.

In the name of the Wounded Healer,

David W. Mann, Pastor
Sunnyslope Mennonite Church
Phoenix, AZ 85020

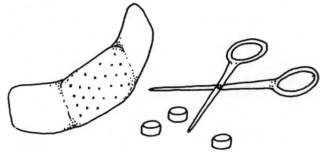

The Good Samaritan Response

For the prayer corner:
A Band-Aid and other items from a first-aid kit.

But a Samaritan while traveling came near him; and when he saw him, he was moved with pity. (Luke 10:33)

Read Luke 10:25-37.

The man was walking from Jerusalem to the city of Jericho, nearly twenty miles away. It was known as a dangerous road, twisting and turning among desolate and rugged hills which were the homes of thieves. A band of bandits attacked him on a deserted stretch of road. They stole his clothes and vanished into the hills. Bruised and bleeding, the man lay half dead by the side of the road. Unless someone came soon to help him, he would surely die.

The priest was the first to come along. While he could preach to others on how to live a godly life, it was an entirely different matter when faced with actually walking in the footsteps of the holy Scriptures. He deliberately walked past an opportunity to serve God in mankind. Instead, he covered his head with fear and probably pretended the man was dead. As so pointedly illustrated in this parable, the priest was unable to take off his long robes of prejudice and deal with the reality of the situation.

The second man was respected by others in the synagogue, but in private the temple official quickened his steps, trying not to look at the body of the wounded man. Both men were interested in worshiping God and belonging to a religious organization, but they missed the importance of identifying God's wonderful work for us to do in our daily life.

Things have not changed much in two thousand years. People who practice a formal religion in a church building often find that living their faith by Christ's example is a challenging job. When asked the question, "Who is your neighbor?" a modern-day Christian might blindly ask, "What neighbor?"

In the area of sexual abusers and victims of sexual abuse, the church has chosen to close its eyes tightly and say, "But we don't have those kind of people here." Facing the reality of sexual abuse in our families is painful for us as individuals and as a church. However, since sexual abuse happens in religious and non-religious families alike, the church can no longer remain silent about the problem.

The church must become the good Samaritan, bringing the balm of education, compassion, and justice to the suffering victims as well as to the abusers. Permission must be given for people to speak of sexual abuse and incest. The church can promote healthy relationships within families. The church can teach respect for children, their rights, and their feelings. It can provide support to families where personal boundaries have been violated through sexual abuse. And adults must become aware of their responsibility as caregivers and protectors of children.

Facing the pain of abuse takes courage, courage that the church is called to demonstrate. Theological and pastoral issues involving obedience, repentance, forgiveness, justice, and reconciliation need to be addressed. Together pastors and the congregation (the church) can become the healing agent by the way they respond to family's suffering from sexual abuse. The church is called to be the good Samaritan in every decade.

The Man from Samaria

1. *Stopped his donkey.* Church members need to stop and address the hidden crime in our midst. Patterns of family terror are repeated again and again in hundreds of thousands of homes each year, making family violence an insidious killer of body and spirit in our midst. Yet for the most part it goes unrecognized, especially by the churches. Christians can no longer look the other way or pretend there are no victims in their congregations. Christians have to stop denying that the problem exists.

2. *Went to help the wounded man.* The church needs to extend their hearts and outstretched hands to both the victim and the abuser. In so doing the church and the individuals will have to honestly confront their feelings about incest and sex in general so that they can more comfortably deal with actual cases. They need to be able to talk openly and comfortably about sexuality.

3. *He bandaged his cuts and bruises.* The church needs to learn first aid for families experiencing sexual violence. When the church accepts the challenge to be involved in the process of restoring health to the individual and the family, it may mean putting the individual before the unit. As with any emergency medical treatment, the immediate needs must first be met. The first bandage to be applied for any victim of sexual abuse is protection. Even if we are not required by our particular state's law to file a child-abuse report, we may still feel an ethical duty to make this response in order to minimize the chances that the sexual violence will continue.

4. *Lifted him on the back of the donkey.* The churches need to recognize that abusers and sexual abuse victims often need assistance in seeking the aid they need. It is unrealistic to think that a dysfunctional family can work out its own problems. Especially in the case of incest, it will be necessary for the sex offender to leave the premises where the victim is living until sufficient therapy has taken place by both the victim and the abuser.

5. *Set off to find an inn.* The church needs to have the resources available to pastoral counselors and others involved with abusers and sexual abuse victims. Having a referral source can be helpful, since families confronted with sexual abuse will not have the presence of mind to take steps toward finding an appropriate therapist.

6. *Stayed the night and nursed the man.* The church needs to support abusers and sexual abuse victims. Some churches sponsor safe houses for victims of domestic violence. Other churches have prison ministries where they bring hope and encouragement to sex offenders.

7. *Paid the bill for both of them.* The church needs to be generous with its gifts of time, talent, and money to meet the needs of the abuser and the sexual abuse victim. Perhaps a special monthly offering can go toward an emergency fund for families during the initial crisis period after the sexual violence has been disclosed.

8. *Promised the innkeeper money until he was well again.* The church needs to be a place where abusers and victims come for healing. It should purchase reading materials on sexual violence for their libraries and can also provide a room where self-help groups for sexual violence can meet. If there is a sexual abuse therapist in the congregation, perhaps that member could offer initial counseling scholarships for an abuser or a sexual abuse victim. Or several churches could share the cost of hiring a therapist for a seminar to address the needs of abusers or survivors of sexual abuse.[19]

Let It Begin with Me

O God,
open my eyes
to see
someone in need
of your
loving touch.
Amen.

TWENTY-NINTH DAY
And Justice for All

For the prayer corner: A key.

*The days are surely coming, says the Lord, when I will raise up
for David a righteous Branch, and he shall reign as king and deal
wisely, and shall execute justice and righteousness in the land.*
(Jeremiah 23:5)

Gloria had been a good girl and kept Daddy's special secret. But
in reality, she couldn't wait to get out from under his control and
go away to school against his wishes. Once she was free from his
advances, she never returned to the family farm. Her brothers
asked if there was a problem because she never came home for
the holidays. She denied there was anything wrong. She said that
as an emergency room nurse, she felt more married to her job
than her family. And another year passed between Gloria and her
father without a confrontation.

Gloria married Solomon, a hardworking man, and she success-
fully kept the secret hidden from him. However, she participated
in sexual relations with him only when she had to. Most of the
time she was angry after sex. It almost seemed an accident that
they had a child at all.

At church Gloria often led the singing in morning worship. She taught a class to refugee families in their community. No one suspected by her words or outward appearance that she was an adult molested as a child. In fact, many women envied Gloria and her example of living the kingdom plan.

That's what caught the congregation by surprise when Gloria and nine-year-old Rebecca came to church one Sunday without Solomon. Gloria looked like she had not slept for days. The pastor inquired if there was a problem. He invited Gloria into his office to offer his support and help.

"Solomon was removed from the house by the police because I caught him doing dirty things to Rebecca in the shed," Gloria said as she kept her eyes cast on the floor. A silence dropped between them and Gloria whispered, "It's exactly the same thing my awful daddy did to me, only no one ever took him away 'cause no one ever knew about it."

Both Gloria and Rebecca were marred by parents who used their parental power and authority to commit sins of sexual violence. This abuse violated the respect, safety, and protection which should exist between children and their families. Instead, these children lose the little power they have to shape their own lives. The opportunity to grow and to learn within a trusting relationship is destroyed by the action of the offender. This is the essence of injustice to its victims.

The healing process began when Gloria was able for the first time in her life to name her abuser. Justice-making begins with truth-telling. A victim who begins to remember and acknowledge experiences of childhood sexual abuse and is ready to speak about these experiences to someone—that person is on the way to becoming a survivor.

Stumbling Blocks to Justice-Making

The primary goal of a response to sexual contact between a child and a significantly older person is to make justice in the midst of injustice. Many times we unconsciously contribute to stopping justice because we don't want to listen to the truth. In doing so, we have done a great injustice.

Please identify the injustice you may have said or done to victims of sexual abuse:

[ ] Is it possible to remember things you experienced when you were three years old?

[ ] That happened a long time ago. You must get on with your life. Forgive and forget.

[ ] How could a child cause so much upheaval and jeopardize the family's future over something that happened twenty or thirty years ago?

[ ] The child must have lied about the behavior of the stepparent because the family is reunited again.

[ ] I don't think the offender has a problem. I think the offender just made a mistake.

[ ] An adult could never willfully exploit a child sexually, especially an adult related to a child.

[ ] I can't believe that no one knew what was going on in that family. The mother must have known about the child's sexual abuse and thus colluded with the offender.

[ ] The state could not prove beyond a reasonable doubt that a crime occurred. That means the accused is innocent.

[ ] How can we send a person to prison just on the statement of someone else? Besides, what if the child is lying?

[ ] The defense attorney has obtained acquittal for the accused. Somebody's lying; I'm just not sure who.[20]

Five Steps to Make Justice Happen

Whether we are the victim, the nonoffending parent, the friend, the helper, or the offender, we do not expect that everything will be just like it was before. But we want it to be made right in some way. We believe the brokenness which resulted from the acts of sexual abuse will somehow be made whole. Some experience of justice is necessary for healing to take place, in order for the victim to become a survivor.

As the truth-telling unfolds, survivors who confront their offenders often struggle against self-blame and guilt. They may also be dealing with their own internal resistance to what they may view as a desire for revenge or punishment. Even after many years, survivors may harbor ambivalent feelings and strong emotional bonds toward the offender. But it is not revenge to tell the truth or to seek justice. It is not punishment to expect restitution. Calling the offender to account is a way of taking back control. It is an opportunity for healing for both the survivor and the offender.

Step 1: *Justice-making may mean truth-telling.*
[ ] Breaking silence about your secret.
[ ] Be willing to talk about your personal experiences with sexual abuse.
[ ] Telling your story to someone who may not want to hear what you have to say (the other parent or relative).
[ ] Telling your story to someone who may not believe you (someone who does not believe the abuser is capable of hurting children).

Step 2: *Justice-making may mean confrontation.*
[ ] With the offender (if he or she is still available).
[ ] With those who knew about the abuse but did not help the child.

Step 3: *Justice-making may mean calling those responsible to account.*
[ ] A letter expressing the victim's pain and anger.
[ ] A direct conversation or confrontation.
[ ] A civil suit filed against the offender.

Step 4: *Justice-making may mean providing restitution.*
[ ] Provide for the expenses of therapy or medical care resulting from the childhood abuse.
[ ] A concrete action the offender does as an attempt to restore wholeness within the survivor.

Step 5: *Justice-making may mean supporting the process of forgiving and letting go.*
[ ] Once some form of justice is experienced, then a victim/survivor can be free to consider forgiveness.
[ ] It is a conscious act of saying that the survivor will not allow the power of the memory of abuse to continue to limit her/his life and thus revictimize her/him each day. It puts the memory in perspective.[21]

Justice When Repentance Is Absent

A victim's desire to confront the offender usually carries with it the expectation that the offender will acknowledge his offense and ask for forgiveness. Such a confession would prepare the way for some form of reconciliation. However, this seldom happens. An adult survivor must be prepared for disappointments when confronting the offender.

The offender may deny that the abuse ever took place and may even be unwilling to discuss the matter at all. A victim should be prepared for this disappointment. Nonetheless, the victim has done what she/he needed to do in confronting the abuse. If the offender is dead or living in an unknown location, there is no opportunity for confrontation. In the absence of repentance or restitution by the offender, justice cannot be served by the legal system alone. It is a shared task of the whole community.

When the offender is unavailable for confrontation, justice-making is done by the wider community:

- The community needs to create an atmosphere in which persons feel safe to speak.

- The community needs to listen and hear the victim's experiences.

- The community needs to believe the victim's experiences.

- Someone needs to express on behalf of the wider community that what occurred should never have happened.

- The community needs to support the process of truth-telling.

One Church's Response

The Social Justice Committee at Bethany Church felt the need to address the injustices of sexual abuse. They identified sexual abuse as acts of violence against innocent victims. Their goal was to bring justice and peace to those in their community who were abusers, victims, or parents of victims of childhood sexual abuse.

They met with their pastor and presented their justice-making

152

plans. In addition, they asked for his full support by preaching a sermon on sexual abuse to the congregation before they implemented their programs. The pastor was reluctant at first. However several members of the committee felt strongly that sexual violence must be identified and disarmed by nonviolent means. The pastor decided to pledge his support and he told the Justice Committee he would preach the sermon.

The committee's action plan consisted of each member taking responsibility for a specific step in the justice-making process. One member volunteered to find a guest speaker for a sexual abuse awareness and prevention clinic which would be free and open to the public. Other churches in their community would be encouraged to attend.

Another member of the committee felt that victims and their parents needed prayer, support, and encouragement. She volunteered to start a prayer line for these parents and also for adults who were sexually abused as children. Many people were surprised when the pastor announced the new prayer chain. There were others, the victims and their families, who were greatly encouraged because finally the church was giving them permission to talk openly about the abuse.

One member of the group was involved in prison ministry. In an effort to support the recovery of offenders and the work of the chaplains who assist in their treatment, the committee agreed to spend the first ten minutes of each meeting writing letters of encouragement to them. This was an ongoing ministry.

The reader in the group volunteered to research materials on sexual abuse and make suggestions for purchases to the church library. He included books on sexual abuse prevention for parents. He wrote book reviews and put them on the bulletin board next to the prayer chain flyers. Later he designed a brochure showing the reading material on sexual violence available on loan from the church library.

One of the mothers who was a Sunday school teacher said it would be impossible to add additional information to the Sunday morning program. So they targeted midweek services and later vacation Bible school to include outreach to the neighboring community. Using visual aids, games, puppet shows, and other educa-

153

tional material, they taught the children how to identify injustices and ways to become peacemakers.

There was a counselor on the Justice Committee, but he did not feel adequately trained to assist sexual abuse victims. He talked to sexual abuse therapists in the area and found one who would come for a small fee to lead a short-term therapy group. In addition, he started a referral file for the pastor and pastoral care workers. He printed a flyer with names of therapists, organizations, and hot lines for any family caught in a cycle of violence and posted it on the Peace and Justice bulletin board.

The adult education teacher was asked to get materials together to explore in greater depth issues of violence and forgiveness. At this time, the church had no known victims or survivors of abuse, but the committee felt the national statistics were accurate and knew members of their community had been victims of sexual violence. The Sunday school teacher was hesitant and counter-offered to teach a class on sexual relationships in a Christian marriage. The Justice Committee was delighted and offered to supply him with materials on possible injustices between the sexes and injustices in the sexual relationship.

The Lenten focus that year was on small groups which processed the collective loss people experienced and explored connections between grieving and birthing. The pastor led a Lenten prayer service incorporating a burning service where everyone was invited to write down and burn a secret wound they had been hiding.

Bethany Church is a prime example of what a handful of peacemakers can do when they dedicate themselves to addressing violence in our world with weapons of nonviolence. They have made justice in the midst of injustice for the abusers, the survivors, and the families. May God richly bless their efforts.[22]

Do I Have to Forgive the Abuser?

For the prayer corner: A packet of flower seeds.

When they came to the place that is called The Skull, they cruci-fied Jesus there with the criminals, one on his right and one on his left. Then Jesus said, "Father, forgive them; for they do not know what they are doing." (Luke 23:33-34)

To Golgotha they took people who committed crimes against others and society. It was nothing more than an ancient death hill for criminals. People, especially those who were taken advantage of and harmed by another, came to watch the hideous method of execution. Many survivors of crimes had feelings of satisfaction that justice was being served. Even if that justice meant taking the life of another.

As Jesus hung from his throne on that awful tree, the blood of sorrow and love dripped from his body. The young rabbi shocked the crowd who gathered when he prayed that God would pardon the sins of his killers. Even for those things that well deserved his anger. Jesus' final teaching was a ten-word lesson. It broke the Jewish law, "an eye for an eye, and a tooth for a tooth" (Exodus 21:24). He taught through example and words: "Father, forgive them; for they do not know what they are doing."

The Bible does not tell us that the person from whom the thief stole was standing in the crowd. But let's suppose he was. Imagine the victim's surprise when Jesus pardoned even the thief who was being crucified with him. If that wasn't shocking enough, Jesus invited the thief to be *with him* in paradise! (Luke 23:43).

I can imagine myself protesting that action, "Wait a minute, Jesus, you don't understand. That man is a thief. He committed a crime. He never told me he was sorry for what he did. In fact, he never paid me for the goods he stole."

A child sexual molester *takes* as a thief. The offender *takes* the innocence, the privacy, that can never be returned or replaced. The sexual perpetrator is also a thief, and a violent one at that.

Yet Jesus, the Son of God, did not seek vengeance against others because of their evil behavior. Forgiveness is never earned or deserved—it is *freely given*. Forgiveness is *for giving*. Jesus offered them—even those who had not repented—forgiveness through the cross.

Thus began the contrast: the example of our Lord's forgiveness on one hand, and on the other hand our reluctance to forgive in the real world as we relate to each other as human beings. We find especially difficult those offenses we consider *unforgivable actions* that affect us personally.

The church has dictated traditional theological understandings on the issue of forgiveness. However, far too often when victims have turned to the church to speak about the unspeakable—violence and sexual abuse in the family—a theology of submission often dictated that a wife or child should return to the very person and place of violence. A premature forgiveness was quickly suggested, and this allowed and accepted the violence. Victims were asked to excuse the perpetrators of their actions. Such insensitive procedure whitewashed the victims' needs with a coat of "forgive and forget." The result was that victims were denied their rights, even the right to express their anger and rage over the injustices that were occurring in their lives.

While the church has announced forgiveness, so often we believers have not learned the practical how-to's in living a lifestyle of forgiveness—especially toward the fallen fellow member. Too often we want vengeance and punishment rather than learning how to help the sex offender. The perpetrator may also be a survivor of childhood abuse. Yet such offenders need to claim responsibility for their own actions, understand the consequences of their behavior on victims, accept forgiveness, make repentant changes, and rebuild their lives.[23] They need our help.

If anyone needs to soul-search their hearts, it is the church at large. The church did not identify the sins of sexual violence. In denying the problem, it failed by not encouraging and assisting perpetrators—some of them pastors—to get into treatment programs designed for sex offenders. In addition, it failed to protect those precious brothers and sisters and those innocent children who survived crimes of violence.

There are some within the community of faith who are willing to reexamine ideas of forgiveness, peace, and reconciliation which decree that past hurts be quickly and quietly forgotten. "I'm quickly moving in the direction of seeing forgiveness in terms *of intent,* and a way of *opening the issue* rather than closing it," said Isaac Block, a pastor and counselor presently researching domestic abuse among Mennonites in Winnipeg, Manitoba.[24] Others need to respect the whole therapeutic process through which the survivor of sexual abuse is going. Each person's timing needs to be honored, even if they never reach the point of forgiving. God recognizes one's desire to forgive, and there may be a long way to travel to accomplish it.

Today pastors and therapists are both in agreement that forgiving is essential to a complete healing. Together they caution survivors and those people who love and support the survivor in recovery. They warn against glibly declaring forgiveness for the abusers too soon in the healing process. First the survivor needs to explore the memory of the abuse and come to a fuller understanding of the abusive events and emotions.

Therapy can help to ease the pain and release the anger, preparing the way for forgiveness. This much is clear from clinical experience: as the issues are being opened, so are the emotional time bombs that have been hidden in secret darkness for years, perhaps even decades.

It is important to recognize your right and your child's right to thoughts, feelings, and emotions, no matter how strong they are and no matter how vengeful your thoughts may be. Your emotions need to be respected and owned. They are yours! Even the strong feelings of anger and hatred toward the child molester and those people who failed to protect the child. With the help of a therapist, families are able to release, experience, and understand feelings of rage, hatred, betrayal, abandonment, sadness, and fear. Such a release makes way for the healing process.

This does not mean that a parent of a sexually abused child will never feel these emotions again because they have worked through them. You will never forget what happened to your child, and at times you may be revisited by angry or blaming feelings. When the anger resurfaces, recognize that it is a normal response to your child's abuse. Allow yourself to feel anger, without acting on it in an unhealthy way. As you communicate your feelings in acceptable and healing ways, you are breaking free from the past and its control over you. The memory of your child's abuse is no longer allowed to limit the quality of life you and your family experience today. You are finally free from the nightmare and its effects upon you and your family.

In her book *Reach for the Rainbow,* Lynne D. Finney, a survivor and therapist, answers the question many adult survivors ask: Do I have to forgive my abuser?

"Certainly not, if by 'forgive' you mean condone what your abuser did to you. 'Condone' means to overlook, and you can never overlook conduct that caused the magnitude of suffering you have endured. Nor can you forget it. Those acts are irrevocable and have affected your life just as your height and coloring affect your life.

"But that does not mean that your abuse has to haunt you or be the focus of the rest of your life. You can let go of what happened and you can let go of the bitterness, anger, and pain you feel about what happened and about your abusers without condoning what they did. 'Letting go' is the true meaning of forgiveness. You are not a God who absolves people of their 'sins.' You can only refuse to harbor the hate and bitterness which will ruin the rest of your life. Forgiveness is not for your abuser, it is for you.

"Forgiveness does not mean putting yourself in a position where someone can harm you [the survivor]. And 'letting go' does not mean you have to talk to the people you forgive again, unless you want to. It is your choice. You can see them if *you* (the survivor) really want to and if you feel safe. The purpose of forgiveness is to help *you* feel better so you will allow yourself to be happy" and to have peace of mind. It is also a redemptive act, taking away your enemy's power over you and releasing the abuser to change for the better, with God's help.[25]

Many who have walked the way of forgiveness have told us the line that was drawn between *"us and them"* has now become a circle including both the abusers and the survivors. Between them are the words our Lord taught us, "Forgive us our trespasses, as we forgive those who trespass against us."

To say, "I cannot tolerate your choice of behavior," does not prevent you from saying, "I forgive you—as a person." To love persons for who they are, does not mean one has to love their choices of behavior. "I forgive you and do not hold your deeds against you—while at the same time I do not condone or tolerate your evil behavior." God loves each person, whether that one's behavior is good or bad. We are called to live in that character.

Scripture gives wise counsel: "Be angry but do not sin; do not let the sun go down on your anger, and do not make room for the devil." Anger is a God-given emotion. The surge of anger is what drives men and women to accomplish great things, to make needed changes. In itself, the anger emotion is neither good nor bad.

The sin may come in how we choose to express the anger. Some thought and delay is wise: "Be . . . slow to speak, slow to anger." Do we have concern for what is right in God's eyes, or do we have a prideful anger which "does not produce God's righteousness?" After inner processing, we may feel led to speak the truth to our neighbor in love and even with strong feelings. We give room for the devil when we nurse anger until it becomes settled hatred toward the abuser and stifles our own lives. We grow in truth and spiritual strength when we deal with our circumstances and relationships and move on with the Spirit's power.[26]

How to Identify False Forgiveness

In the book *Caring Enough Not to Forgive*, David Augsburger gives us some insight into false forgiveness.[27]

• When "forgiveness" puts you one-up, on top, in a superior place, as the benefactor, the generous one, the giver of freedom and dignity—don't trust it, don't give it, don't accept it. It is not forgiveness: *It's sweet saintly revenge.*

• When "forgiveness" is one way, calling one person to accept the difference, absorb the pain, adjust to injustice—don't rush to it, don't close the case with it. It's not forgiveness: *It's loving submission.*

• When "forgiveness" distorts feelings by denying that there was hurt, disconnecting from feelings of pain and squelching the emotions that rise, pretending that all is forgiven, forgotten, forgone—don't trust it. *It's a mechanical trick.*

• When "forgiveness denies that there is anger, acts as if it never happened, smiles as though it never hurt, fakes as though it's all forgotten—don't offer it. Don't trust it. Don't depend on it. It's not forgiveness. *It's a magical fantasy.*

• When "forgiveness" ends open relationships, leaves people cautious, twice shy, safely concealed, afraid to risk free, open spontaneous living, don't forgive. It's not forgiveness. *It's private alienation. It's individual estrangement.*

How to Identify True Forgiveness

In the book *Caring Enough to Forgive*, David Augsburger gives us some insight into true forgiveness.[28]

• *Forgive by realizing wrongdoing.* I see you as a wrongdoer. I feel injured, innocent, exploited, abused. I am pointing the finger

160

of blame. Any movement toward forgiving begins with recognizing that we are in this pain together.

- *Forgive by reaffirming love.* I see you as an evildoer. I feel hurt, resentful, angry, demanding. I am refusing to see that in spite of wrongdoing you are an equally precious person of worth, value, dignity. Forgiveness begins as I see you again with love.

- *Forgive by releasing the past.* The past exists only in memory, consequences, effects. It has power over me only as I continue to give it my power. I can let go, release it, move freely. I am not my past. The future is not yet. I can fear it, flee it, face it, embrace it, and be free to live now.

- *Forgive by renewing repentance.* Forgiveness is renewed repentance. The real enduring issues of justice, integrity, and the righteousness of right relationships are resolved and restructured into the restored relationships. So we are free to love, live, and risk again.

- *Forgive by rediscovering community.* In a world of flawed communication, community is possible through understanding others. In a world of painful alienation, community is created by accepting others. In a world of broken trust, community is sustained by forgiveness.

The following chart shows the path toward healing, recovery, and restoration of right relationships. This can happen through the grace of God and our openness to let his forgiveness transform our lives (Mark 11:25).

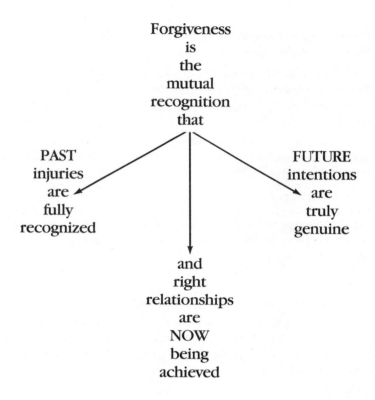

Forgiveness
is
the
mutual
recognition
that

PAST
injuries
are
fully
recognized

FUTURE
intentions
are
truly
genuine

and
right
relationships
are
NOW
being
achieved

Toward a Forgiving Attitude

To work toward having a forgiving attitude, here are some practical steps tried by others. Some may be difficult, but they are worth trying, with God's help.

• Norman Vincent Peale, in his book *Inspiring Messages for Daily Living*,[29] suggests that one of the first prayers to offer is for the grace to pray for the person against whom the unforgiving feelings are directed. This is important, for at the beginning of the process, you may feel that it is hypocritical to pray for that offender. But if you pray for the grace to do so, you will be lifted to a new level of spiritual understanding and strength.

• Christians around the world have personalized the Lord's Prayer, particularly for the petition of forgiveness. "Forgive me of my sins, as I forgive (the offender's name) who has sinned against us."

• Recognize that forgiveness is a process and not a one-time act. Our Lord told us to forgive "seventy times seven." Do not become discouraged.

• A letter-prayer may assist you to express the emotions you feel for the offender in a safe environment. Address a letter to the offender, telling how you feel about the past and how that person has hurt your family. Put the letter in a envelope and seal it. As you tear the letter up, repeat this prayer:

Prayer to Forgive

O God, our lives have been torn and broken by the actions of this person. Whatever is broken in that one's emotions and life, I ask you to restore and heal. Alone, I am too broken to forgive, but through your strength I forgive (name the person). Amen.

THIRTY-FIRST DAY
An Understanding Heart

For the prayer corner: Two paper hearts and a rock.

When they make a long blast with the ram's horn, as soon as you hear the sound of the trumpet, then all the people shall shout with a great shout; and the wall of the city will fall down flat.
(Joshua 6:5)

Seven years have passed since our child broke down the wall she was hiding behind and told her *secret* to us, her parents. Her father and I are grateful for the courage she has shown by working through *some* of the hurt she carries. Our family gains strength from God, who weeps along with us; from Jesus, our Wounded Healer; from the Holy Spirit, our Comforter; and from many caring and understanding Christian friends.

With the assistance of therapy, we have all learned to communicate with each other more effectively. It continues to be difficult for me to listen to her story and see the pain she carries. Yet the unfortunate experience resulted in our child confirming that her parents were a safe place to take her troubles, and they would believe and protect her. They also assured her that she was not responsible for her molestation or any resulting problems in her family. Even though a bad thing happened to her, she knows she is not a bad girl. In fact, she is a wonderful girl that had some sad things happen to her when she was little.[30]

I hope that, by the time my child grows up, attitudes will have changed toward sexual abuse. Currently society and the church's response could be compared to Jericho, the great city keeping itself carefully guarded from the truth about sexual abuse behind its steep walls of ignorance.

Lynne Finney is a survivor and therapist who carries the "ark" of research as a modern-day Joshua. Recent studies report that *80 percent* of fathers who commit incest have been sexually or physically abused as children.[31] Finney notes that many people who molest children learned their behavior by being abused themselves as children. Thus they pass it on from generation to generation.

It seems beyond human comprehension how childhood victims of sexual violence could be capable of passing on that affliction to other innocent children. This is an incredible fact, perhaps too shocking to accept and understand. The children of Israel continued to circle the city of Jericho seven times, waiting for the wall to fall. So too must we continue to work hard to break down the wall of ignorance and denial surrounding sexual abuse and those who abuse innocent children.

In her book *Reach for the Rainbow*, Lynne Finney sounds the trumpet of truth: "Abuse is the number one sickness that is sweeping across our country. Abuse does not occur in happy families; it occurs in dysfunctional families where the members' needs are not being met. And it occurs in families where one or more members have themselves been abused in childhood but have not worked out their past pain." Abusers are people in need of help.[32]

That information helped me break through the judgmental feelings I harbored against child molesters. I did not know the personal childhood history of the person who betrayed our child. Yet I now know that, given the choice, what human beings in their right mind would chose to bring lifelong pain to another? Only persons in pain themselves—persons in need of help.

Slowly I began to separate the person from the acts of sexual abuse. That was not an easy task because the person never said he was sorry for the harm he brought my child. Now I realize that was an impossible request because his illness by nature caused him to deny his problems. Sadly he was denied the treatment he needed because he was never held accountable for the offenses he committed.

As the emotional wall fell inside of me, it was replaced with compassion and understanding for the offending person. Our relationship with him remains broken, but I no longer hate the man. I simply hate his choice of behavior toward innocent children.

I hope and pray that the day will come when each one of us can accept our responsibility in the complex issues of sexual abuse. Only when we are willing to work together will we be able to break down the barriers between us and work collectively against the number-one epidemic in our church community and in our country. This must involve the survivor, the offender, each member of a loving church or congregation, and each member of society, all of whom have contributed to the myths surrounding sexual abuse.

* * *

A Letter of Caring

Dear (name of offender),

You and I have something in common. We have both shared in the life of this child. Although you knew her when she was little, now she has grown up quite a bit. Most of the time she is a normal teenager. She likes to listen to music, talks on the phone with her friends, and loves pizza.

Deep inside of her, in a place that her friends do not see, she carries a hurt that was given her by you. A hurt that violated the trust she put in you. By your words and actions to her, you opened a special part of her that was meant to be saved until she was older. I am so sorry that you were not able to control your behavior.

It frightens me to know that you have never taken responsibility for your behavior. You even walked away from the scene of the crime, leaving no evidence proving you were a child molester. Perhaps if someone had held you to account for your actions, you might have felt the guilt and sorrow that would have enabled you to get the medical and psychological help you need. There are many caring professionals who can assist you in a successful sexual abuse treatment program.

If there is anything we can learn from the past, it should be to take the past and use it to make a better future. Our children can live in a safer world if those people who are hurting them can find the courage to seek the help they need. I know it won't be easy, but I'm just asking you to try.

I pray that you will be convicted by God's Spirit with an all-compelling need to discover the freedom and peace that results from facing the misuse of your God-given sexuality.

(Your name), the parent of (child's name)

* * *

Prayer by a Sex Offender[33]

Dear Lord, it's been so long since I felt like praying. So much has happened, and I'm so ashamed.

Here in prison, I feel so alone, so abandoned, so worthless, so bitter and empty. Through your Holy Word, you tell us to bring all our burdens to you in prayer. You also said we should pray for others. I am burdened about many things and persons.

Oh God, I confess my sin—what I did was so wrong. I ask first for my own forgiveness. And, then I ask for grace to learn to forgive.

Be especially close to the one I wronged. Give her your love and understanding. Let her understand and believe what happened wasn't her fault. Lord, grant her healing and above all, peace of mind.

For those who, in their piety, became so angry with me—grant to them a great measure of compassion, that they may yet become a support system for those of us who have fallen.

For my beloved pastor, I pray for wisdom. Give him new insight about the great gulf between the need to uphold the dictates of the holy fathers about discipline and doctrine, and the ability to lead the flock in the practice of compassion, forgiveness, and redemption. I felt I could not share with him my sin and my shame, for it would surely compromise his role.

Dear heavenly Father, I pray for the church. May you grant courage to come out of the dark ages of ignorance and denial; to courageously offer families permission to learn together the sacredness of our human sexuality; to learn, in the context of the household of faith, how to deal forthrightly, honestly, and openly with the expressions of our God-given sexual feelings and desires—that beat in the hearts of everyone; to teach us the ability to face the negative issues around our oft-misused sexuality, with the power of your Spirit.

Oh God, attend to the physical, emotional, and spiritual needs of my family. They have suffered much because of my behavior. Especially, minister to my beloved wife. She has suffred more than me in her zeal to remain faithful to her vow: in sickness and in health; in success and in adversity. Lord, hold her close to you, that her faithfulness to you not falter because of me.

For my brothers and sisters who have fallen from grace through misuse of their sexuality, I pray you'll send someone to minister healing and understanding without judgment. May they discover your forgiveness anew.

Then for family members of the many victims of sexual misuse, I pray earnestly for their ability to find healing for their confusion around how a loving God could allow their child to be unprotected. Help them to look beyond blaming you—for what I and others have done.

Dear Lord, my heart cries out in agony that you will answer my prayer, in your own way and on your own time schedule. Amen.

A Litany of Acknowledgment

By Kelly Jarrett,[34]
Based on 2 Samuel 13:1-21

Leader:

Now Absalom, David's son, had a beautiful sister, whose name was Tamar. After a time Amnon, David's son, fell in love with her. Amnon was so tormented with lust that he made himself ill because of his half sister Tamar. She was a virgin, about twelve years old, and it seemed impossible to Amnon to do anything to her because she was guarded in the royal house.

Congregation:

We acknowledge the Tamars among us, beautiful sisters, deserving love, and living in danger. For them we give thanks and ask protection.

Leader:

But Amnon had a friend whose name was Jonadab, the son of

169

Shimeah, David's brother. Jonadab, a crafty man, said to Amnon, "O son of the king, why are you so haggard morning after morning? Will you not tell me?" Amnon said to him, "I am lovesick for Tamar, my brother Absalom's sister." Jonadab said to him, "I have a plan. Lie down on your bed, and pretend to be ill. When your father comes to see you, say to him, 'Let my sister Tamar come and give me bread to eat, and prepare the food in my sight, so that I may see it and eat it from her hand.' "

Congregation:
We acknowledge that there are those among us, trusted friends and family, who plot and scheme against our vulnerable children.

Leader:
So Amnon lay down and pretended to be ill. When the king came to see him, Amnon said to the king, "Please let my sister Tamar come and make a couple of cakes in my sight, that I may eat from her hand." Then David sent a message home to Tamar: "Go to your brother Amnon's house, and prepare food for him."

Congregation:
We acknowledge the pain and conflict of parents who, like David, are deceived, manipulated, and caught in webs of collusion.

Leader:
So Tamar went to her brother Amnon's house, where he was lying down. She took dough, kneaded it, made cakes in his sight, and baked the cakes. Then she took the pan and emptied it out on the table. He could see and smell the cakes, but he refused to get up and eat. Then Amnon said to his manservant, "Send out everyone from me except Tamar." So everyone went out from him. Then Amnon said to Tamar, "Bring the food into the bedchamber, that I may eat it from your hand." And Tamar took the cakes she had made, and brought them into the chamber to Amnon her brother.

Congregation:

We acknowledge the trust of our children and their desire to please us. We grieve that these qualities, born of their love and dependence on us, place them at risk. We acknowledge the compounding of this risk by secrecy and isolation.

Leader:

But when Tamar brought the cakes near to Amnon to eat, he took hold of her, and said to her, "Come, lie with me, my sister." She answered him, "No, my brother, do not force me. Such a thing is not done in Israel; do not do this sacrilege. As for me, where could I carry my shame? And as for you, you would be as one of the scoundrels in Israel. Now therefore, I pray you, speak to the king; for he will not withhold me from you. For you, his firstborn, the king would arrange a marriage, even against the rules." But Amnon would not listen to her; and being stronger than she, he forced her and lay with her.

Congregation:

We acknowledge the realities of violence and violation that are forced on our children in secrecy. We acknowledge the courage and resistance of those who, in the face of superior strength and deaf ears, have few options and little hope of protecting themselves. We respect them for speaking out in protest.

Leader:

Then Amnon was seized with a very great loathing for her; his loathing was even greater than the lust he had felt for her. And Amnon said to her, "Get out!" But she said to him, "No, my brother; for this wrong in sending me away is greater than the other that you did to me." But he would not listen to her. He called the young man who served him and said, "Put this woman out of my presence, and bolt the door after her." So his servant put her out, and bolted the door after her.

Congregation:

We acknowledge the guilt, anger, and hatred of those who abuse our children and recognize that these feelings are often projected onto our children. We acknowledge that in the rejec-

171

tion and banishment of child victims, the cycle of victim blaming comes full circle.

Leader:

Tamar was wearing a long robe with sleeves; for thus were the virgin daughters of the king clad of old. She put ashes on her head, and rent the long robe which she wore. She laid her hand on her head, and went away, crying aloud as she went. And her brother Absalom said to her, "Has Amnon your brother been with you? Now hold your peace, my sister, for he is your brother. Do not take this to heart." So Tamar dwelt, a desolate woman, in her brother Absalom's house.

Congregation:

We acknowledge that all too often, when victims break silence and in grief, shame, and desolation reach out for help, they are counseled to hold their peace. Thus the circle of secrecy and denial widens. We acknowledge the Tamars among us, beautiful sisters, violated, grieving, and desolate. For them we give thanks and ask healing.

All:

We acknowledge the pain and suffering of all persons, child victims, adult survivors, family members, friends, and offenders, who are affected by child sexual abuse.

Leader:

Let us examine our hearts and our actions and ask God's forgiveness for the times when, through word, silence, deed, or inaction, we have added to the burdens of pain and suffering caused by child sexual abuse.

Notes and Credits

1. Englewood Cliffs, N.J.: Prentice Hall, 1950, 1987.

2. Kathy Woods, *Victims Are Not Guilty* (Fullerton, Calif.: R. C. Law & Co., For Kids Sake, 1989); used with permission.

3. "A Liturgy for a Lost Childhood," by Marty Green, reprinted with permission from *Daughters of Sarah* (September/October 1987), 3801 N. Keeler, Chicago, IL 60641; also in the packet "Broken Boundaries: Resources for Pastoring People (Child Sexual Abuse)," MCC Domestic Violence Task Force, copyright 1989 by Mennonite Central Committee US (MCC), Akron, PA 17501.

4. Kathryn B. Hagans and Joyce Case, *When Your Child Has Been Molested: A Parent's Guide to Healing and Recovery* (Lexington, Mass.: D. C. Heath and Company/Lexington Books, 1988), p. 145.

5. Adapted with permission from "Dynamics in Incestuous Families" and "Victims Rarely Lie" in the packet "Broken Boundaries," MCC.

6. Adapted with permission from "Victims Rarely Lie," in the packet "Broken Boundaries," MCC.

7. Adapted with permission from "Victims Rarely Lie," in the packet "Broken Boundaries," MCC.

8. A letter taken from the file of a sex offender serving a prison term for sexually molesting his daughter. He wrote this letter to her as part of his treatment process. Her name is changed. Used with the courtesy and permission of Theron Weldy, Psychotherapist, Phoenix, Arizona.

9. Phyllis Trible, "Tamar: The Royal Rape of Wisdom," in her book *Texts of Terror* (Philadelphia: Fortress Press, 1984), pp. 53-54.

10. Ibid., p. 49.

11. Ibid., p. 49; see Genesis 2:25; 3:7.

12. Based by permission on "Incest Survivors' Twenty Reasons for Telling Their Stories," *Women's Concerns Report*, no. 83 (March-April 1989), MCC.

13. Reprinted by permission from *Silent Scream*, by Martha Janssen, copyright 1983, Fortress Press, Philadelphia, Pa.; also in the packet "Broken Boundaries," MCC.

14. A letter taken from the file of a sex offender serving a prison term for sexually molesting his nephew. This abuser had been sexually molested as a boy. As part of his treatment, he wrote this letter to the man who had molested him. The name is changed. Used with the courtesy and permission of Theron Weldy, Psychotherapist, Phoenix, Arizona.

15. These advocacy tips are based by permission on "Incest—You Can Make a Difference," *Women's Concerns Report*, no. 83 (March-April 1989), MCC.

16. Excerpted with permission from Marie M. Fortune's *Sexual Violence: The Unmentionable Sin* (New York: The Pilgrim Press, 1983), chapter 3. Reprinted as "Sexual Violence: Reframing the Ethical Questions" in the packet "Broken Boundaries, MCC.

17. Used by permission of the author, David W. Mann, Phoenix, Arizona.

18. *Gospel Herald* 84 (September 27, 1988): 658-659.

19. This interpretation and application of the good Samaritan story is adapted by permission from "Child Sexual Abuse," "The Hidden Crime in Our Midst," and "A Pastoral Response to the Incestuous Family," in the packet "Broken Boundaries," MCC.

20. Adapted with permission from "Pastoral Sexual Abuse, One Congregation's Ordeal" and "Victims Rarely Lie," in the packet "Broken Boundaries," MCC.

21. Adapted with permission from "Making Justice" in "Broken Boundaries," MCC.

22. Adapted with permission from "Making Justice," "Responding to Child Sexual Abuse," and "Pastoral Sexual Abuse: One Congregation's Ordeal," from "Broken Boundaries," MCC.

23. Note the creative efforts by the Victim Offender Reconciliation Program (VORP), John Longhurst, "Sex Offenders . . . ," *Mennonite Weekly Reivew,* Feb. 14, 1991, p. 3; cf. "Members Abused . . . ," May 9, 1991, p. 2. More information is available through MCC.

24. Quoted by Don Ratzlaff, "Shedding Light on Darkness of Violence in Our Midst," *Mennonite Reporter* 20, no. 24 (Dec. 10, 1990), p. 3.

25. Lynne D. Finney, *Reach for the Rainbow: Advanced Healing for Survivors of Sexual Abuse* (Malibu, Calif.: Changes Publishing, 1990), pp. 103-108.

26. See Matthew 5:43-48; Ephesians 4:25-27; James 1:19-20.

27. Part 2 of his book *Caring Enough to Forgive* (Scottdale, Pa.: Herald Press ed., 1981 copyright by Regal Books), especially pp. 8, 24, 38, 52, 66.

28. Ibid., summary of part 1 with chart from p. 71; used with permission.

29. See note 1, above.

30. See the helpful treatment of these aspects in *When Your Child Has Been Molested* (note 4, above).

31. Frank Pittman, *Turning Points* (New York: Norton, 1987), p. 308.

32. See Lynn D. Finney, *Reach for the Rainbow.*

33. This prayer was shared by a sex offender serving time in prison for child sexual abuse. He had nearly completed a year of intensive treatment and reported renewing his experience of faith. Used with the courtesy and permission of Theron Weldy, Psychotherapist, Phoenix, Arizona.

34. Prepared by Kelly Jarrett, Coordinating Council for Children in Crisis, Inc., New Haven, Conn., and adapted by permission from *Working Together* 8, no. 4 (summer 1988), a news journal published quarterly by the Center for the Prevention of Sexual and Domestic Violence, 1914 N. 34th, Suite 105, Seattle, WA 98103; included in "Broken Boundaries," MCC.

The Author

K. C. Ridings was born in Elkhorn, Wisconsin, and lived all of her formative years in the Midwest. Her mother believed strongly in Sunday school attendance. After graduation from high school, Ridings enrolled in Lutheran Bible Institute in Minneapolis. This enriched her strong roots in the Word of God.

The following year the first of her six children was born. Several years later she and her husband, Joseph, had two more sons. Then, in an effort to expand their family, they adopted their daughters Marisol and Angelica from El Salvador in 1983. In 1988 Dobson Ranch awarded her Mother of the Year, Second Place, in Mesa, Arizona. Joseph won Father of the Year, First Place.

Ridings has been able to use her gift of writing in women's ministries. For one year she led a women's Bible study and later wrote and led weekly prayer services for forty women. She enjoys teaching religious education to kindergarten children.

Since 1986 Ridings has been a member of Tempe Christian Writers Club. Frequently her inspirational articles are featured in Saturday's religion section of the Phoenix area *Tribune*.

K. C. Ridings lives with her husband, Joseph, and their children in Mesa, Arizona, and is a member of the local Queen of Peace Roman Catholic Church. From her home she answers a Christian Parents Help Line for Sexual Abuse. She may be contacted through Herald Press for speaking appointments.